The CATCHER

The CATCHER

Baseball Behind the Seams

EMMIS BOOKS
1700 Madison Road
Cincinnati, Ohio 45206
www.emmisbooks.com

Library of Congress Control Number: 2005920005
ISBN 1-57860-164-9

Edited by Jack Heffron
Cover and interior design by Stephen Sullivan

Photos courtesy of Mark Rucker and Transcendental Graphics
except where indicated.
Front cover photo © Reuters/CORBIS

The CATCHER

Baseball
Behind The Seams

ROB TRUCKS

CINCINNATI, OHIO

DEDICATION

For Manny Sanguillen, Tony Peña and Mike LaValliere

THANKS

Thanks, of course, to all the catchers who so generously provided time, conversation, and insight.

Thanks, also, to the people at Emmis Books, Kevin Behan and Monica Pence of the Baltimore Orioles, Eric Phillips and Katie Kirby of the Chicago White Sox, Cliff Russell and Molly Light of the Detroit Tigers, Arthur Richman, Rick Cerrone and Ben Tuliebitz of the New York Yankees, Kristy Fick of the Oakland Athletics, John Blake of the Texas Rangers, Jay Alves of the Colorado Rockies, Warren Miller of the Houston Astros, Jon Greenberg and Jason Parry of the Milwaukee Brewers, Jay Horwitz and Chris Tropeano of the New York Mets, Leigh Tobin of the Philadelphia Phillies, Blake Rhodes of the San Francisco Giants and the media staffs of the Huntsville Stars, Birmingham Barons, New Haven Ravens, Lakewood Blue Claws, Trenton Thunder, Delmarva Shorebirds, especially Larry Glover of the Lexington Legends. A near bottomless pit of gratitude exists for Laurie Mundy, the most supportive and overqualified research assistant in history.

Very special thanks to Karan Rinaldo, Jim Kaat, Taylor Phillips, Will Blythe, John Marvosa, and all who count yourselves as family and friends.

TABLE OF CONTENTS

Reach Masks

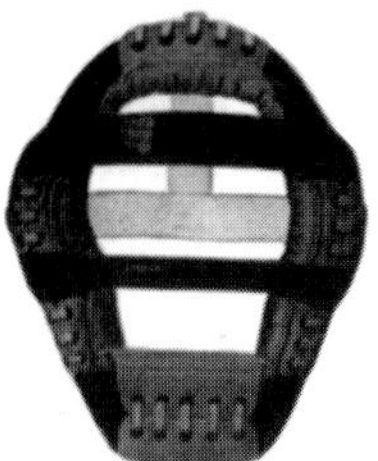

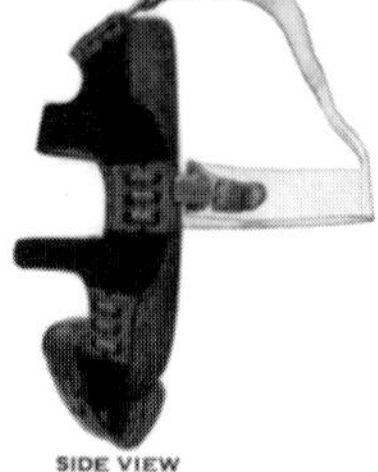

No. JP Each $13.50

No. RU Each $9.00

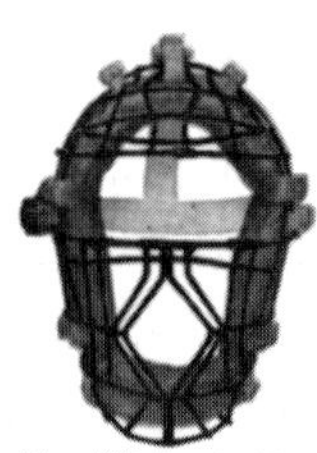

No. 6W Each $7.00

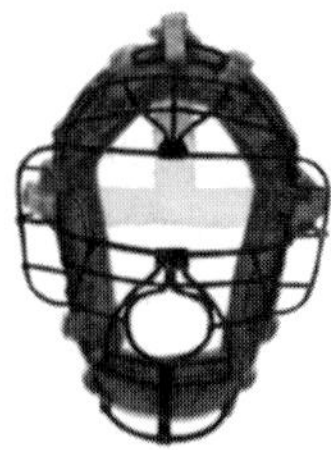

No. SL Each $6.00

CLOSE association with the leading catchers ever since Base Ball became a National pastime, has enabled us to secure the best ideas of those who knew what they required and we have been in a position to keep our masks up to date by incorporating the most practical ideas secured from such sources. We continually seek expert advice in order to maintain the practical utility value of our products.

THE NEWEST AND BEST MASK

No. JP. Mask is in our estimation the most practical face protector ever invented for ball players. Originated and designed by a professional of wide experience. Thoroughly subjected to the most severe tests, it has proven to be the most absolutely safe and perfect type of mask.

The frame is made of one solid piece of light weight, special composition metal, guaranteed to withstand any shock or blow of ordinary use. A particular feature is the light weight, this mask being lighter than the average professional style of wire frame construction. Greater expanse of vision is possible and less shadow in the catcher's eyes. Fitted with the Reach Special full length face padding. These pads are laced to the frame and can be removed or adjusted as may be required.

No. RU. Umpire's Special. Extra strong tempered steel wire. Trussed frame construction with hinged ear pieces and neck protecting extension. Pads are adjustable by means of strap and buckle fastenings. Adjustable head straps.

No. 6W. Professional Model. Finest tempered steel wire. Double frame with cantilever reinforcement wires. This model embodies the "Spitter" and Open Vision features. Sides extended to protect the ears. Pads are adjustable by means of strap and buckle fastenings. The strongest wire mask made.

No. SL. "Spitter." Heavy tempered steel wire with reinforced joints. Extended sides to protect ears. Adjustable pads fastened to frame by means of strap and buckle attachments. Head straps are adjustable.

No. 400. Diamond Special Model. Heavy steel wire. Constructed to embody superior strength and to include the "Spitter" and Open Vision features. Adjustable pads and head straps.

1923 advertisement for catcher's masks

1ST

In the Beginning

This journey, like all journeys, has a beginning. In February 2003, a collection of interviews I'd conducted, *Cup of Coffee: The Very Short Careers of Eighteen Major League Pitchers,* was published, and I spent the opening week of the 2003 baseball season in Ohio and Kentucky on a book tour. On a free afternoon I attended the third regular season game ever held at Cincinnati's Great American Ballpark, a contest won, like the previous two games, by the visiting Pittsburgh Pirates. The next night I was scheduled to be interviewed during the Single A Lexington Legends game by Lexington play-by-play broadcaster Larry Glover. Larry asked if, while I was in town, I would be interested in interviewing Legends' manager Russ Nixon.

During his career, which included twelve major league seasons, Nixon played for the Cleveland Indians,

Boston Red Sox, and Minnesota Twins. He caught Tracy Stallard at Yankee Stadium on the final day of the 1961 season when Nixon's former teammate Roger Maris broke a 0-0 tie by hitting his record-setting sixty-first home run of the year. Nixon also managed the Cincinnati Reds and the Atlanta Braves, and the year before taking the Lexington job he served as the catching instructor for the Pittsburgh Pirates.

I accepted Larry Glover's offer to interview Russ Nixon. I had no book in mind, no agenda to advance. Though I had pitched in Little League, I knew nothing about catching. Catching was a mystery. I nervously smoked cigarettes under the stands of Legends Field waiting for Russ Nixon to arrive that early Monday afternoon, and when he did I followed him into the manager's office. His team had begun the season with one win and three losses in their first four games. Lexington would lose again that night and the next two nights before beginning the year's first road trip. As those young ballplayers set off toward Maryland, I began an exploration of catchers.

Cup of Coffee is a collection of interviews with eighteen pitchers whose entire major league careers lasted less than fifty innings. Though I'd possessed an interest in major league short-timers since first seeing *Field of Dreams,* the project started from an innocent question about my great-uncle, Virgil Trucks.

Virgil was a major league pitcher for seventeen years, one of four men in major league history to pitch two no-hitters in a single season, and I knew his career well. My extremely short baseball career primarily took place on the pitcher's mound, so pitching, as much as anything in baseball, was what I knew. And I wanted, as much as possible, to stay in my comfort zone.

Catchers have no comfort zone. Gnarled fingers from a thousand foul tips and weakened knees from years of squatting are no more uncommon to a catcher than cauliflower ears are to a boxer. If Cal Ripken's consecutive game streak is ever broken, it will not be by a catcher. They are borderline masochists in the line of fire. They are, as former catcher and current Houston Astros bench coach John Tamargo says, "a different breed." No other position on the baseball diamond is as underappreciated or as full of inherent contradiction.

There is a well-recognized phrase to describe the catcher's equipment: tools of ignorance.

And yet, catchers are anything but ignorant when it comes to understanding the game of baseball. They make up a larger percentage of current major league managers than any other position. Former catchers not only guide their teams, they do so with some success. In recent years, Joe Torre's New York Yankees (three times), Bob Brenly's Arizona Diamondbacks, and Mike Scioscia's Anaheim Angels were skippered by former major league catchers.

"Tools of ignorance" is a phrase generally attributed to Herold "Muddy" Ruel who, like Russ Nixon, was a baseball lifer.

Ruel played for nineteen major league seasons and

caught over fourteen hundred games. He played for six different franchises, served as the general manager of the Detroit Tigers, manager of the St. Louis Browns, and assistant to Commissioner "Happy" Chandler. Ruel was the regular catcher for Hall of Fame pitcher Walter "Big Train" Johnson of the Washington Senators and was on the field when Cleveland shortstop Ray Chapman was struck in the head on August 16, 1920 by a pitch thrown by submarining right-hander Carl Mays of the New York Yankees. Chapman died the next day and is the last baseball fatality from an on-field incident.

In the off-season "Muddy" Ruel practiced law and, in fact, argued before the United State Supreme Court, which, by comparison, offers a presumptive explanation of the unfortunate labeling of his baseball attire.

For the television viewer, the catcher is simultaneously both the most visible (thanks to the centerfield camera) and most anonymous (thanks to the catcher's mask) player on the field.

One might compare the catcher to a hockey goalie. Each is covered, head to toe, with padding unique to his position in anticipation of an errant puck or ball. Each serves as his team's last line of defense in guarding his respective net or plate. Catchers, like goalies, look out on the entire playing surface in front of them, but the goalie faces the same direction as his teammates. The catcher faces his teammates.

In baseball, catchers look out in the same direction as the batter (their opponent) and the umpire (the

HEROLD 'MUDDY' RUEL

arbiter). And in this location they experience more contact, both physical and verbal, with each than any other member of their team.

The catcher is much more actively involved in the game than his hockey counterpart. If his teammates are playing well, a goalie might be relatively uninvolved in the action for minutes at a time, and be asked to stop no more than twenty shots on goal in an evening. In baseball, no pitch is thrown until signaled by the catcher, and the number of pitches received during a game is almost certain to pass the century mark.

In hockey, a skater is penalized for running into the goalie. In baseball, a runner rounding third has free reign in his attempt to separate the catcher from the ball.

Why would a sane man volunteer to receive baseballs thrown at speeds approaching one hundred miles an hour? Why would an accomplished athlete place himself in the way of a runner with every legal right to leave him on the ground, a weary aggregate of disconnected parts?

More often than not, catchers are made, not born.

More than any other position on a major league field, the catcher is likely to have begun playing another position. Catchers, as major leaguer Todd Greene points out, are rarely noticed unless they do something wrong. And children, boys, and especially athletically talented boys, like to be noticed. Which is why it's not surprising that the better Little League athletes often gravitate to more visible and less physical positions, say third base or shortstop or pitcher, where not only their strong arms can be utilized, but their play can be seen as well.

On the off chance that a young athletic boy does choose to play catcher, parents often might provide resistance. Catching is relatively dangerous. From foul tips to plays at the plate, the likelihood of physical contact, and therefore injury that might stunt a promising career, increases when a child gets behind the plate.

All four living Hall of Fame catchers—Yogi Berra, Johnny Bench, Carlton Fisk and Gary Carter—started at other positions.

Russ Nixon is an exception to the rule.

"I've got a twin brother," he told me that Monday afternoon in the manager's office. "There was only the two of us. My grandfather was a very good semi-pro player. We were farmers, so the games were only played on weekends. The little old towns there in southwestern Ohio had their local teams, and all of them were pretty good players so we watched those games as kids. My grandfather wanted his twin grandsons to be ballplayers.

"My grandfather wanted one of us to be a pitcher and one to be a catcher, so Roy was the pitcher and I had the catcher's mitt. I don't know why I wanted to catch. I mean, it just so happened that I had the catcher's mitt and I never did anything else. Roy didn't want to catch, I know that. I don't recall having anything but a catcher's mitt, but I know my grandfather bought both gloves."

Sometimes the selection of a position is accidental, or not really a selection at all. Sometimes it's just the quickest way into a game.

Bart Zeller played in one game for the 1970 St.

YOGI BERRA is one of the four living Hall of Fame catchers (Johnny Bench, Carlton Fisk and Gary Carter are the others) to start at a position other than catcher.

Louis Cardinals, and like the now famous Moonlight Graham, never got the opportunity to bat. His decision to play catcher took about as much time as it took for him to start and finish his major league playing career.

"I remember when I was eight years old," Zeller says, "and the coach said, 'All right, everybody that wants to be a third baseman, go to third base. Everybody that wants to be a pitcher, go to the pitcher's mound. Everybody that wants to be a first baseman, go to first base.' And hell, I had no idea, so when they got all done throwing guys out to positions I was still standing there, and he said, 'All right, you can be the catcher.' "

For Ned Yost, now manager of the Milwaukee Brewers, catching was a way to participate in his neighborhood game managed, like all neighborhood games, by the older kids.

"When I was a kid," he says, "we would get together and play baseball games on our block. We had eight or ten kids that would play, and nobody wanted to catch. I was a little bit younger than some of them so I said, "I'll catch." So I would catch in the baseball games on our block.

"When I got into Little League I was nine years old. There was no catcher on the team, and the coach asked if anybody had ever caught before. I said that I had done it. I caught on my block. There was the birth of a catcher. And I'll never forget, the only advice he gave me was, 'Son, don't ever turn your head. Keep your head straight forward. If the ball's in the dirt, don't look away. If he swings, don't turn away. Keep your head straight.' And I've caught my whole life."

At least on the major league level, catcher Otis Thornton's career was similar to that of Bart Zeller, but the way he became a catcher, a decade before and thousand miles away, nearly mirrors that of Ned Yost.

Thornton caught both Don Wilson and J. R. Richard in the Astros' minor league organization before playing in his first, his second, and his last major league games for Houston on July 6, 1973. Both of Thornton's parents passed away before he turned thirteen, so he lived with his aunt and uncle in the town of Dolemite, Alabama.

"Within our community," Thornton says, "we didn't have a catcher. We had to wait until some players came from Ohio, Donny and Lonny. Donny was the pitcher and Lonny was the catcher. And so we were waiting on them to come for the summer so we could get started. And they were late coming, so when Lonny came I said, 'Do you blink your eyes to catch the ball?' He said, 'Sometimes.' So that next year he was slow about showing up, so I got back there. We didn't have a catcher, and here we've got a game and nobody to catch. So I said I'd get back there. So I got back there. Catching is fun."

Pirates' catcher Humberto Cota also thought catching would be fun.

"I was six," he says, "and I wasn't playing that much, and I just wanted to get dirty and just kind of tell my friends I played baseball. I played today. And I felt the easiest way to get dirty is catching, you know. That's how I decided."

Alabama native Frank House played ten seasons as a major league catcher, primarily with the Detroit Tigers, and like Otis Thornton (and former major league catchers Mike O'Berry, Charlie Moore, and Buddy Hancken) grew up outside of Birmingham.

"I was raised out in Bessemer. That was an iron ore mining and steel manufacturing town, and all the companies had a ball team. And Daddy was managing the industrial team, Muscoda, in the little mining community where we lived. There was a series of iron ore mines and limestone mines there that were used to make converted steel, and there were certainly a lot of outstanding baseball players that played with those teams. Of course, Daddy being the manager, all the equipment always came back to our house when the game was over. Daddy was a pitcher, and I never will forget the old black catcher's mitt there. It was so stiff you could not have bent it with a circle saw.

"I was, I don't know, five or six, seven or eight years old, I guess, when he threw me that mitt, and I'd get out in the yard and I'd catch him. He would show me how to catch the ball—above your waist one way, and you turn the mitt over to catch it below there—and if you don't do it right the chances are the ball's going to bounce off the glove and hit you right in the nose. And it did that, and I think the only words he uttered as he walked down there to see if I was ever going to stop bleeding was, 'What did I tell you, boy? I told you about that, didn't I?' He never had to tell me again. I understood now. So from that I started catching."

Baseball, of course, is the sport of fathers and sons.

If you won't allow me the romantic, the ideal, the literary (see: *The National Pastime, Field of Dreams*, Donald Hall's *Fathers Playing Catch with Sons*), then grant me the practical. Of the three major American sports, baseball uses the smallest ball. Children—boys or girls—can grasp a baseball, throw a baseball, catch a baseball, years before their hands are big enough to throw a football or shoot a basketball. Playing catch, even if it consists of simply rolling a ball across the floor to a waiting toddler, is an activity most participate in at a very early age.

Many take it to a higher level.

There have been eight pairs of fathers and sons to catch in the major leagues. The earliest duo was Connie Mack, considered one of the finest managers in baseball's history, and his son, Earle, who also became a manager after catching one game in 1910 (one might suspect nepotism at work from the circumstantial evidence). Next came Billy Sullivan Sr. and Billy Sullivan Jr. Billy Sr. was also a manager, but favoritism doesn't seem to have factored into Billy's career, which lasted from 1931 to 1947.

Another father-son, Senior-Junior combination, the Earle Bruckers, follows. Earle Sr. was also a manager (see a trend here?), though only for five games in 1952, which was three games longer than his son's 1948 playing career lasted.

Sam Hairston, the first African-American ballplayer signed by the Chicago White Sox (most likely the reason his major league career was so short), caught two games for the ChiSox in 1951. His son Jerry played parts of fourteen seasons for the White Sox as an outfielder, and his grandson, Jerry Jr., is a second basemen with the Orioles, but Sam's son John caught one game for the crosstown Cubs in 1969. John was the backup to longtime Cub catcher Randy Hundley, whose son Todd caught in the major leagues for fourteen seasons.

Utilityman Ozzie Virgil Sr. was most frequently positioned at third base, but he did manage to catch thirty-five major league games. His son, Ozzie Jr., caught nearly seven hundred games and made the National League All-Star team in 1985 and 1987.

Haywood Sullivan was drafted by the Red Sox, caught for the Red Sox, served as general manager and part-owner of the Red Sox, but managed the Kansas City Athletics in 1965. His son Marc, a second-round draft pick of (who else?) the Red Sox in 1979, was a defensive specialist, playing in the field in every single one of his 137 games over five major league seasons, and finishing with an average below the Mendoza Line.

The final father-son catching duo presents, debatably, the most successful catching son of all. Jason Kendall's father, Fred, broke in with the expansion San Diego Padres in 1969 and finished his career there (with one season away in Cleveland and one in Boston) in 1980. Jason, of course, was a first-round draft pick of the Pittsburgh Pirates in 1992, just days before his eighteenth birthday. Four years later he was the Bucs' everyday catcher. In his nine major league seasons to date he's been selected to the All-Star team three times and has a career batting average of over .300.

Of course, not everyone has the talent or opportunity to make it to the major leagues. Johnny Bench's father, Ted, who installed his youngest son at the catcher position, played catcher during the service.

Four-time Gold Glove winner Charles Johnson's

father was a pitcher, playing college ball alongside Andre Dawson at Florida A&M. Johnson was coached by his dad at Fort Pierce Westwood High School, but the younger Johnson began his Little League career in the outfield. As he says, "It got boring. I decided I wanted to be part of the action. I went home and my father said, 'This is what you want to do?' I said, 'Yeah.' He said, 'Okay. Let's work at it.'"

As the high school coach, Johnson's father had access to baseballs and a pitching machine.

"He would bring the pitching machine home," Johnson says, "or I would go to the school and he would set it up, and I'd block baseballs on Saturdays and weekends. He'd speed the machine up, and I'd get closer and closer and closer to the machine, where it'd help my reflexes as far as my catching and receiving. We'd do that a lot, and he would hit me in the face with baseballs with the mask on so I wouldn't blink my eyes.

We would do a lot of footwork, a lot of blocking. He would bring the machine home, and I had a tool shed right behind me. I was blocking. The balls that did miss me would hit the tool shed and eventually, over a period of years, it busted a big hole in it, so the goal was not to let the ball go into the hole anymore."

Other conversions to the catcher position are not only numerous, but they often come later in a career.

Buddy Hancken, a one-game catcher for the Philadelphia A's in 1940, took over the catcher position in a trial by fire.

"I was playing ball in Alexandria in the Class D

league," Hancken says. "We only had one catcher, and he got his hand broke. We were all around home plate and the manager looked around and said, 'Who's going to catch?' Nobody said a word. I said, 'Let me catch.' He said, 'Did you ever catch?' I said, 'No, but I'll catch until you get somebody.' Well, I caught the rest of the year. And the next spring Detroit sent me down to Lakeland, Florida and Mickey Cochrane was the manager, and he worked with me for about four or five days, and then sent me back up to the Evangeline League, and that's where I caught."

Randy Hunt played parts of two seasons with the Expos and Cardinals in the mid-eighties.

"I was actually a shortstop in high school and drafted as a shortstop," he says, "and when I got to junior college, we needed somebody. I think our catcher got hurt and we needed somebody to catch. So Chat-tahoochee Valley is where I started actually catching. We just needed somebody to be a catcher that year."

Keith Osik, who played for the Baltimore Orioles in 2004 after seven seasons with Pittsburgh and one in Milwaukee, was also converted in college.

"There was a scout with the Diamondbacks who thought I would make a good catcher. I guess he projected me as being a utility player or a catcher. This is while I was in high school. I guess maybe he thought at that time I didn't run good enough. There was something that I guess he saw that he thought I would make a good catcher. Maybe it was the arm strength. I don't know.

"He asked my high school coach if I wouldn't mind

taking some throws, even though I didn't know how to throw the ball to second, as far as being a catcher. I just did the best I could and threw it down there.

"I was a shortstop my first two years at LSU, and then I played third my junior year. We needed to get another bat in the lineup, and I said to my manager that I might be able to catch. I think catching was probably going to be my opportunity to get there because you start seeing guys that are a little bit quicker than you coming up through the ranks."

Current Chicago Cubs catcher Michael Barrett has a theory formed by his own playing experience and an older brother's knee injury. Barrett suggests that newer conversions from the left side of the infield might actually have an advantage over players with adolescent ex-perience behind the plate.

"I started out at other positions. I think it's key for a catcher to have played other positions to get a better understanding of what's going on around the field. Most catchers, nowadays, are converted middle infielders or converted infielders. I think the reason for that is because the face of the game has changed in a lot of ways. The catcher nowadays is required to have as much foot speed as some of the other position players, or as close to it as they can get, and usually that comes from former infielders. Quick hands and the arm strength of some shortstops, some third basemen are a positive for a lot of catchers.

"What I am saying is that as levels go up and up it's tough for guys who have been catching their whole life. I think it's tough for kids who've had knee trouble from catching so many games to continue on with their career when you have guys that are being converted at the freshman level who have never caught and their legs are fresh. I think that's probably the benefit of having a converted catcher over someone who's been catching.

"I would try to keep my kid from going into catching as much as I could until the last possible minute. And the reason for that is because it's such a physically demanding position. It is the best position on the field, I feel, as far as learning the game, but at the same time, it's very difficult on the body and anything can happen."

For many players who convert to the position after turning pro, it's not so much about matching their physical skills to the position as it is about simply advancing their career. If a conversion is to happen, it often occurs after the player's first year of professional play. Barrett signed with Montreal in 1995 and had spent his entire career in the Expos organization before being traded following the 2003 season.

"When you get into professional baseball your goal is to make it to the major leagues," Barrett says. "And it's not easy at the minor league level to predict what's going to happen.

"In my case I was a shortstop, and at the time we had Orlando Cabrera, Hiram Bocachica and Jason Camilli. We were loaded with shortstops, as far as the organization was concerned. At third base we were also loaded. We had Shane Andrews, Izzy Alcantara and a guy named Jose Hernandez, and they really felt like the depth behind the plate was weak considering we'd lost Darrin Fletcher. We picked up Chris Widger along the way, but in our minor league system we had very few catchers that they felt were major league talent. So when they presented the idea to me, I really felt like it was a great opportunity to catch and to make it to the big leagues faster.

"I thought the way they handled it was really good. They gave me an opportunity my first year to get comfortable in professional baseball, to play a full season at shortstop. That way, I get settled into my professional career, and then at the end of the season they decided to tell me that they wanted me to be a catcher."

Adam Melhuse was drafted as a third baseman by the Toronto Blue Jays in 1993 and had his first cup of coffee in the majors in 2000 with the Dodgers. He served as a utility man for the Rockies in 2001 before finding a spot on the Oakland A's roster during the 2003 season. His ability to play a variety of positions, including catcher, has made a major league career possible, but that doesn't mean he didn't initially harbor doubts about the change.

"I got drafted at third base," Melhuse says. "My freshman and sophomore year at college I was a shortstop, and then my junior year I played third base. But in the instructional league they asked me to try catching.

"I was with the Blue Jays. It was the end of the first week of instructional league, and Mel Queen, who was the minor league director at the time, sat me aside and said, Hey, listen. This is what we'd like you to do. I mean, this is instructional league. There's no statistics. This really is almost like a glorified practice, so there's no pressure. We'd like you to try it. The fact that you've been an infielder all your life, you have good hands. You've got a strong, accurate throwing arm. The fact that you can switch-hit doesn't hurt your chances at all. We'd like for you to give it a try.

"At the time I had a bunch of emotions. One was like, What's the matter? They didn't like me at third base? Okay, if this doesn't work out I'm out of baseball already. Just a whole lot of different thoughts, you know. And then, I gave it a shot. I mean, what was I going to tell them? Just say, No, that I didn't want to do it? I thought that'd be the worst thing I could do so I strapped the gear on and went right over to the bullpen ten minutes after we had our conversation. The next thing I know I'm there catching bullpens, and I've got a catcher's glove on and I'm just thinking, What the heck is going on?

"But I stuck with it all instructional league, and they were happy with how things progressed. After that, when I came back for spring training, I told myself that as long as I keep moving up I'll stick with the catching. When I got home my dad and friends of my dad that were associated with baseball were saying, "Hey, we think it's a great move. This could really help you out and really get you up there a lot quicker."

"You look at the third basemen in the league. They're all hitting thirty, forty, maybe fifty home runs at the time, and I definitely wasn't that kind of power hitter. And I was too slow to move back to shortstop or even second base so I figured, Why not? Let's give it a shot. Let's just put a hundred percent effort into it, and I made the progression each year. I repeated the Florida State League, and then made the jump to Double A. Like I said, as long as I was going to make the step up the next year then I was going to stick with it. And everything kind of went as planned."

2ND

The Loathing of Johnny Bench

The summer before I entered seventh grade my family moved to a new house in Birmingham, Alabama. Another family, though not as new to the neighborhood as ours, were also recent arrivals. Like us, their family consisted of a mother, father, and three children—Joan, Jerry, Jennifer, Jeff, and Jeannine. They had come to Alabama from Indiana, and they talked funny.

Jeff, the middle child, was my age. We played ball together on the street, got in trouble together (the worst of it involving BB guns, water balloons, and automobiles). Later we took turns driving each other to high school. My baseball playing days were over by this time. When Little League gave way to Babe Ruth League, I didn't make the jump. Jeff was an outfielder on the high school baseball team and later played four years for Harry "The Hat" Walker at the University of Alabama at Birmingham.

The Youngs were Reds fans. I had grown up a Pirates fan, though to this day I have no idea why. I was in my early thirties before I had so much as changed planes in

JOHNNY BENCH congratulated by teammates Cesar Geranimo and Tony Perez after hitting a homerun.

Pittsburgh. In the seventies, the Pirates and Reds more or less dominated the National League, and on more than one occasion the teams faced each other in the National League Championship Series.

The Pirates, winners of the National League East, lost to the Reds, winners of the National League West, in the 1970 Championship Series three games to none. In 1972 the Pirates lost to the Reds in the Championship

Series three games to two. The Reds scored two runs in the bottom of the ninth inning of Game Five, the last one on a wild pitch by Pittsburgh's Bob Moose, to advance to the World Series. The Pirates missed the playoffs in 1973, their first year without Roberto Clemente since 1954, but returned to the Champ-ionship Series in 1974, losing to the Dodgers.

The Reds were back again in 1975 and beat the Pirates for the third time in five years, three games to none, on their way to winning the World Championship in what many consider to be the greatest World Series ever played.

When the Reds won an important series—I first remember this happening in 1970—various members of the Young family, Jeff and at least one of his parents for starters, would go out on the deck behind their house and beat pots and pans together. Literally. They would yell and cheer and bang those pots and pans in a way never before or since heard in that neighborhood. You would've expected such a reaction in Times Square on New Year's after the ball dropped.

The Pirates-Reds rivalry mattered. It was personal.

Pittsburgh, though a strong team throughout the decade, didn't win their division again until 1979. They beat the Reds in the League Championship Series for the first time in four tries, but both Jeff and I had left for college by that time. When the Series was played, he was in Birmingham for spring baseball drills, and I was in Mobile participating in my one and only college cross-country season. Payback had been denied.

The Youngs owned one pet, a twenty-pound housecat named J.B. The initials stood for Johnny Bench. I didn't like the cat, and I didn't like Johnny Bench. But now I must admit that Johnny Bench is the greatest catcher in my lifetime. Johnny Bench is the most important catcher in baseball's long history. Johnny Bench changed the way we look at the position of catcher.

Bench was taken in the second round in professional baseball's first amateur draft in 1965, and the second catcher selected overall. Ray Fosse, who would later make baseball history in a collision with Bench's teammate Pete Rose, was the first. Bench was called up to the major leagues in 1967 and was the Reds starter by 1968. Over the course of his seventeen major league seasons Bench caught 1742 games. He was the first catcher ever selected as Rookie of the Year, in 1968, and made the All-Star team every season from 1968 to 1980. He won the National League Most Valuable Player twice and the World Series MVP once.

Offensively Bench led the league in home runs twice, in total bases once, and RBI three times despite never playing in a full slate of games, and he retired having hit more home runs as a catcher than any other player. But he is possibly best known for his defensive prowess, including possessing one of the strongest catching arms of all-time.

Though Elston Howard was the first to use a hinged catcher's mitt, and Cubs catcher Randy Hundley began using it in the majors before Bench was called up for good, it was Bench who truly popularized the glove and the resulting one-handed catching technique that has been employed ever since. He was the first catcher to wear a protective helmet in the field. Perhaps Bench's greatest defensive achievement is his ten Gold Glove Awards at the catcher position, a record considered unattainable until it was recently matched by Ivan Rodriguez.

It pains me to say all this because I don't like Johnny Bench. To be fair, I've never met the man. I'm judging him in advance, all the way back to my childhood. I hate Johnny Bench the same way Red Sox fans hate Bucky Dent.

Both Don Werner and Mike O'Berry were backups to Johnny Bench. Werner arrived, briefly, in 1975 but didn't stay with the club until injuries to Bench began to curtail his time behind the plate. By the time O'Berry left Cincinnati, Johnny Bench was primarily a third baseman.

If he is not already, Werner will one day be the answer to a trivia question. In 1978 he was on the receiving end of the only major league no-hitter thrown by Hall of Famer Tom Seaver. Werner's major league career lasted a total of 118 games over the course of seven seasons, five with Cincinnati. In 2003 he was a coach for the Delmarva Shorebirds in the single A South Atlantic League. We talked in the sun-drenched left field stands one afternoon before batting practice in

Lakewood, New Jersey.

Werner, like Bench, was drafted by the Reds out of high school, and while many young prospects might be disheartened to learn they'd been selected by an organization with a future Hall of Famer at their position, Werner was enthusiastic about the possibility.

"I got picked by the Reds in the fifth round," he says. "Johnny Bench was my favorite player. We're not really that far apart in age, but I just loved watching him catch, and it was kind of exciting to think I was in the same organization as he was, that I could learn a lot from him.

"Bench came on the scene, and I saw him doing all the things that I liked doing as a catcher—picking guys off base. I loved the way he used his arm, the way he moved around back there. He's just so impressive, so imposing back there. That was the position and this was the way it was supposed to be played and that's the way I wanted to play it too.

"He never really went to his knees to block balls," Werner says. "You talk to anybody about catching and they're going to say, 'Go to your knees to block the ball.' He very rarely did because he had great hands. He had the ability to do things other catchers couldn't do. One thing that he did well was his exchange. He had a great exchange and he had the great power. You see so many catchers, and they don't combine the great exchange and the power. You see them have one or the other but not both."

"As far as power goes," Werner says, "he had one of

those balls that looked like it was going to bounce to second, and then it would have that carry and go right through the base. That's how I judge a catcher's arm today. Is the throw going through the base, or is it pretty much done when it gets to the base? If that base was another three to five feet behind, would that still have been a good throw? You don't see many guys throwing the ball through the base anymore, and that's all part of the exchange, the way they use the hinged glove, the way their footwork is. If you give them the ball and have them throw down to second base they'll show a pretty good arm, but you don't see many catchers throw through the base. They don't have the exchange and they don't have the footwork where they're using all the power they have."

The exchange that Don Werner is talking about is switching the ball from the glove hand to the throwing hand, not necessarily a skill that non-catchers or non-coaches would notice.

"I compare it to an infielder catching a ground ball," Werner says. "An infielder doesn't catch a ground ball with his glove and then bring it up to where the glove's to the ear. He gets it out. The exchange is done out front. You'll hear a lot of guys say, 'Catch the ball and bring it up to your ear,' but when that happens the ball should already be out of your glove. That way you get the full arc of your arm. You get the opportunity, if you don't have the seams, to get the seams. A lot of guys catch the ball with their glove and they'll bring it right up to their ear, and that doesn't work. It's just like an infielder.

"You get a fluid process by the exchange. If your exchange is done with your glove, and then you bring your glove back to your hand up high by your ear, you're not going to have a very good exchange. You've got to get it over to your bare-hand side, but out front. If I told you to take a baseball and throw it over the center field wall, would you have your hand up here by your ear and then start your throw? Or would you have it more out front where there would be kind of a fluid motion? That's the position you've got to get into. You can't bring the ball back up by your ear, make an exchange, get the seams and then have a strong throw to second. The chances of that are slim. You've got to be absolutely perfect to do something like that. This way there's a little margin of error because you've got the full arc of your arm. You have an opportunity to get the seams, and even a good catcher, probably eighty percent of the time, has the seams just the way he likes it when he throws it to second, and that's a very good guy. But that's what gives you the opportunity to get the seams, by getting the ball out of the glove and into your bare hand right away. That's the first thing you want to do.

"I think his footwork was pretty good. When he was going towards second base he had everything going that way, and he wasn't stepping behind himself or just pivoting and throwing. He had very nice footwork."

It's possible that Johnny Bench was so good at what he did—scooping balls rather than blocking them, his good footwork, his exchange, his unbelievable arm—that kids attempting to emulate him might've undermined their effectiveness because they didn't have the skills to do the things Bench did the way Bench did them. Without Bench's quick hands, those kids were better off blocking balls rather than trying to scoop them (and then having to chase the ball to the backstop).

After taking a much-needed break following his playing career, Mike O'Berry managed in the independent leagues. From there he returned home—Birmingham, Alabama—taking the job of head baseball coach at Pelham High School. His teams consistently reach the state playoffs and have even been nationally ranked.

O'Berry played college ball for the University of South Alabama under Eddie Stanky before being drafted by the Boston Red Sox in 1975. By 1979 he had reached the majors with the Sox. Carlton Fisk was hurt that season and O'Berry worked as the backup to Gary Allenson, a rookie. Allenson hit .203 in 241 at-bats. O'Berry caught in forty-three games for the Red Sox that year, and batted a mere .169 in fifty-nine at-bats.

The following year O'Berry was traded to the Cubs. He caught nineteen games as a sub for the switch-hitting Tim Blackwell, who had his career year, catching in 103 games with a .272 batting average.

O'Berry's lack of offense (he batted .208 in 1980) seemed to take his new team by surprise, because when the 1981 season opened O'Berry was with Cincinnati.

When I met him on a late spring morning, the Pelham High School parking lot was alive with activity, until eight o'clock when classes started and everything outside the building grew quiet. The morning dew was still on the baseball field, and O'Berry led me into a large, concrete-block building behind the bleachers on the right-field side of the high school ballpark. The structure was carpeted with AstroTurf and housed a batting cage, a locker room and the coach's office. The place was dark until the florescent lights flickered and buzzed before settling into an early morning hum.

"I definitely think my strength was throwing," O'Berry says. "You know, catching and throwing. I was the guy that would get a chance to throw guys out. And I wasn't afraid to throw. Even in the minors I probably led most catchers in errors, but then again I probably led most catchers in picking guys off first, second and third, too, because I threw the ball around a little bit.

"But I think receiving and handling pitchers and understanding that part was probably what got me to the big leagues. Hitting-wise, in high school and college, I was decent. If you go back to my minor league days, I always hit fairly well in April, May and June, but then July and August were always a struggle for me. I never lifted weights in high school or college. Weight programs when I was in high school were non-existent. I was catching 120, 125 games every summer, and I was just not strong enough to do that and still hit. Because hitting's all about creating bat speed, and when you can't create bat speed the results aren't going to be as good as they need to be.

"It was something I realized while I was playing, but then in the same instant I thought, If I start lifting a lot of weights, is it going to hurt my arm? And if I do that, am I going to be able to hit well enough to maintain where I am and not throw as well as I do? It was like, I don't want to start doing something I don't know a whole lot about and end up hurting my arm to where it's going to end my career. If I knew what I know now about weightlifting and stretching and a throwing program I could've gone through that process and not worried about it, but as a high school kid you don't know all this stuff. I have seen guys, even today, who used to throw pretty good and got into a lot of weight-lifting that don't throw very good anymore.

As was the case in Boston, when O'Berry arrived in Cincinnati the star catcher was injured and he was left to support Joe Nolan in the strike-shortened '81 season and Alex Trevino in 1982.

"Johnny caught some that year," O'Berry says, "but really very few games early. I think he caught until Seaver got his 3000th strikeout or whatever, and from that point on I caught all of Seaver's starts the rest of '81 and most of '82. I felt in '81 he should've won the Cy Young.

"But Johnny and I got along good. We played a lot of golf together. He wasn't a guy that was real outspoken, but if you asked him something—when I talked to him about pitching different guys, different hitters and things along that line—he would help."

As it turned out, 1980 would be Bench's last season as a front-line catcher. Though he didn't retire until 1983, the demands of the position had taken their toll. He caught seven games in 1981, one game in 1982 and five games in his final year. By that time O'Berry had moved on to California to serve as the backup catcher to Bob Boone.

Lance Parrish was drafted as a third baseman by the Detroit Tigers in 1974, but when his career ended in 1995 only six men in history had caught more major league games. The all-time record holder, Carlton Fisk, is in the Hall of Fame, as are six of the seven ranked directly behind Parrish—Rick Ferrell, Gabby Hartnett, Johnny Bench, Ray Schalk, Bill Dickey, and Yogi Berra.

"I was a big fan of Johnny Bench when I was growing up," says Parrish, now the bullpen coach for the Detroit Tigers. "He was a guy that I always tried to pattern myself after when I caught. I didn't really follow too many guys that closely, but I admired Johnny Bench."

Bench, of course, worked hard to become the catcher he was. If anything, Parrish, the converted third baseman, worked even harder.

"When I showed up to instructional ball down in Florida," Parrish says, "our farm director, Hoot Evers, said they wanted to move me to catcher and would like me to start working out there.

"They told me that they had no heir apparent to the

catching position in Detroit, that they knew I had a background in catching, and they felt like, with my arm, and I was big, and looked to be fairly durable, that it would be an easy transition for me to make, and they thought that I would make a good catcher. At that time, it was not a big deal to me. I was just a ballplayer, and wherever they wanted me to play that's where I played, and I didn't have any problem with it.

"Obviously," Parrish says, "from that day forward that's all I did, so I guess after a while I just associated with the catching position. That was my job."

Parrish spent the next season in Single A, learning his craft. The following year he played for Detroit's Double A club in Montgomery, Alabama. Former catcher Les Moss was his manager.

"He's the guy that I give almost all the credit to for making me into a pretty decent receiver," Parrish says. "There were a lot of things that I needed to work on, a lot of things that I wasn't aware of that came with the position, and he spent an awful lot of time with me.

"Mechanically, I think, I was not very polished. I let a lot of balls get by me. I was not very adept at blocking balls in the dirt, so that was one of the main areas that we attacked. I had to block a zillion baseballs in the dirt. In fact, there was a time when we switched from Dunedin, Florida, to Huggins-Stengel Field in St Pete for our instructional ball home, and they had a batting cage on the side of the field, and I had to go into the batting cage with a couple of the other guys that were down there, and we had to block balls off of the curveball machine with no glove. He made us get in there with our catching gear and no glove, and the idea behind that was, when you block a ball in the dirt, you're not trying to catch it. You're trying to use your body to block the ball and your glove is just a tool to stick between your legs to plug the hole up, so he made us learn how to block the ball with our body without using our glove. We got beat to death. I had welts all over me when I came out of there. That was just one of the things that, at the time, I didn't really appreciate a whole lot, but I do feel, in hindsight, that it made me a lot better learning how to do it the proper way.

"At home I was on the mandatory extra hitting list," Parrish says, "so I had to come in early every day and work on my hitting, and then I had to come in early every day on the road and work on my catching. So that was a tough year as far as that goes. But you know what? It's very easy for me to look back, and I've said this to a number of people, if it wasn't for Les and all the stuff that he made me do, all the drills that I had to go through with him, all the extra time, if it were not for that I probably wouldn't have made it to the major leagues. I had the ability. It was just all misdirected, and I didn't know what I was doing. He's the guy that refined me well enough to where I could at least get a chance to play at the major league level."

Lance Parrish worked hard, participated in drills that most likely no longer exist in professional baseball, in order to fit the mold created by Johnny Bench's stellar play. Both are large men with offensive power that, at times, drew attention away from their defensive capabilities.

Bench played at 6'1", 208 pounds and hit 389 home runs over the course of his career. Parrish played at 6'3", 220 and registered 324 round trippers.

Bench won ten Gold Gloves at catcher. Parrish won three. Bench was selected to the All-Star team fourteen times; Parrish eight. Parrish played on one world championship team while Bench played on two, and won the World Series MVP in 1976 for batting .533 with two home runs and six RBI in just four games. Perhaps as significant as his offensive statistics in the 1976 Series is the fact that he easily threw out Mickey Rivers, the Yankees best base stealer, in Game One causing the Yankees to settle for advancing base by base for the rest of the short series.

"Bench was a guy who was very well-rounded, obviously," Parrish says. "He was a very good defensive catcher, very good offensive catcher, and that's what I wanted to be. I wanted to be the total package."

3RD

A Catcher's Timeline

October 17
1859

William "Buck" Ewing, the first catcher elected to the Baseball Hall of Fame, is born in Hoagland, Ohio. A great all-around athlete, Ewing played all nine positions on the diamond during his career. He was the first major leaguer to hit ten home runs in a season (1883 with the New York Gothams), averaged .303 for his career and captained two teams (the 1888 and 1889 New York Giants) to world championships. Ewing was known for his strong arm, often throwing out runners from his catcher's crouch. And against stereotype, Ewing was a speedy runner, finishing in the league's top ten in triples nine times and stealing 354 bases over his career. Like many former catchers to follow, Ewing became a major league manager. As a skipper he had a career winning percentage of .553.

1876

Fred Thayer, while managing the Harvard baseball team, gives a modified fencing mask to his catcher to use during the season. This is the first documented use of a mask by a catcher.

1885

Catchers and umpires first use chest protectors.

June 28
1870

May 1
1884

Moses Fleetwood Walker, the major leagues' first African-American ballplayer, makes his debut as a catcher for the 1884 Toledo Blue Stockings. He plays in forty-two games and bats .263.

In a game with the Cincinnati Red Stockings, catcher **Doug Allison** of the Washington Nationals is the first player to wear a glove on the field. All catchers soon began wearing a glove—usually fingerless with padding at the palm—and usually were the only players on the field to wear one until fielders began using them later in the decade.

August 27
1897

"The Duke of Tralee" Roger Bresnahan, the second catcher elected to the Baseball Hall of Fame, makes his major league debut. However, on this day he will pitch a six-hit shutout. Like Buck Ewing before him, the versatile Bresnahan will play all nine positions during his major league career and later manage.

August 27
1907

Bresnahan, then a fiery New York Giants catcher, introduces the shin guard, a modified version of the guards used by cricket players, on Opening Day. Within a few years, all catchers will wear them.

June 28
1907

The Washington Senators steal thirteen bases in a single game against Yankees catcher **Branch Rickey**. This sets an American League record that still stands. It is also Rickey's last season as a player until 1914, when he placed himself into two contests while managing the St. Louis Browns. Rickey, of course, later became one of baseball's most innovative and successful general managers and is perhaps best known for signing Jackie Robinson to a major league contract.

July 19
1915

Once again the Washington Senators set an American League record for baserunning, this time swiping eight bases in an inning against Cleveland catcher (and future manager) **Steve O'Neil**.

September 8
1916

Philadelphia A's catcher **Wally Schang** becomes the first player in major league history to homer from both sides of the plate in a single game. He will hit fifty-seven other home runs in his nineteen-year career.

December 5
1926

St. Louis Cardinals catcher **Bob O'Farrell** is awarded the National League's Most Valuable Player award, the first catcher so honored in either league. After eleven seasons in a Cubs uniform, O'Farrell came to St. Louis, where he hit seven home runs, drove in sixty-eight runs and batted .293 in 147 games, helping the Cardinals to a four games to three World Series victory over the New York Yankees.

April 30
1922

White Sox catcher **Ray "Cracker" Schalk** catches Charlie Robertson's perfect game for a 2-0 win over the Tigers. It is the fourth major league no-hitter caught by Schalk, which is still a record. The catcher for the 1919 team of Black Sox Scandal infamy played eighteen seasons and caught a total of 1727 games, all but five of those for Chicago. Schalk led the league in fielding percentage eight times and in putouts nine times. In 1916 he stole thirty bases, setting a record for American League catchers that lasted for sixty-six years. Schalk also managed, and in 1955 was voted into the Baseball Hall of Fame.

Future Hall of Famer Mickey Cochrane, playing for Connie Mack's Philadelphia Athletics, is the first catcher to be named American League Most Valuable Player. He will win the Award again in 1934, his first year in Detroit and his first season as player-manager. The Tigers will lose a seven-game World Series to the St. Louis Cardinals but will win it all over the Chicago Cubs in 1935. In 1947 Cochrane will be the first catcher voted into the Hall of Fame by the Baseball Writers Association of America.

October 16
1928

August 3
1940

While his teammates play a doubleheader against the Bees, Reds' backup catcher **Willard Hershberger** commits suicide by slashing his throat in the bathroom of Boston's Copley Plaza Hotel. The Reds' starting catcher that season, **Ernie Lombardi**, will also attempt suicide in 1953 by cutting his own throat. The receiver of both of Johnny Vander Meer's consecutive no-hitters, Lombardi recovers from his attempt and lives until 1977, nine years before he is elected to the Baseball Hall of Fame.

October 8
1939

In the fourth and final game of the World Series between the New York Yankees and the Cincinnati Reds, Reds' catcher **Ernie Lombardi** is knocked unconscious in a home plate collision with New York's Charlie Keller. The ball rolls away from him, allowing Joe DiMaggio to circle the bases. This famous moment in baseball history quickly comes to be called "The Lombardi Snooze."

April 21
1946

Frankie Hayes of the Cleveland Indians establishes the record for most consecutive games caught with 312. He began the streak on October 2, 1943 while playing for the St. Louis Browns and continued it through the 1944 season with the Philadepphia Athletics, who traded him early in 1945 to Cleveland.

January 20
1947

September 29
1951

Clint Courtney makes his major league debut as a member of the New York Yankees. He is the first catcher in major league history to wear eyeglasses.

Josh Gibson, the Negro League's greatest power hitter and most famous catcher, dies in Pittsburgh at the age of thirty-five, just three months before baseball is integrated. Nicknamed "the black Babe Ruth," Gibson led the league in home runs for nine seasons and was the second Negro League ballplayer, and the only catcher, inducted at Cooperstown.

September 22
1946

Lawrence Peter "Yogi" Berra makes his major league debut. Berra will play nineteen seasons, win the American League MVP Award three times, and be selected for the All-Star team fifteen times. As a player he will be a part of ten World Series champions, more than any other baseball player in history. He will manage both the New York Mets and New York Yankees and be elected to the Baseball Hall of Fame in 1972.

May 3
1952

Catcher **Quincy Trouppe** and pitcher Sam Jones form the first black battery in American League history in a game between the Cleveland Indians and the Boston Red Sox. The National League's first black battery was formed in 1949.

Clint Courtney is first once again, this time for wearing an oversized mitt designed by his manager, former catcher Paul Richards, to reduce passed balls when receiving knuckleballer Hoyt Wilhelm. The glove is forty ounces heavier and fifty percent larger than a regular-sized mitt. Wilhelm pitches a complete game, 3-2 victory over the Yankees and Courtney allows no passed balls.

May 27
1960

September 29
1957

The final major league game played at Brooklyn's Ebbets Field is also **Roy Campanella's** final game. In January of 1958 he will suffer a broken neck, and his legs will be paralyzed in an early morning automobile accident. Campanella spent seven seasons, beginning when he was just fifteen years old, with the Baltimore Elite Giants of the Negro National League before joining the Dodgers. With Brooklyn he would win the National League Most Valuable Player Award in 1951, 1953 and 1955. In 1953 Campanella set a home run record for catchers with forty-one. He was elected to the Hall of Fame in 1969.

Catcher **Elston Howard** is the first African-American at any position to win the American League's Most Valuable Player Award. A nine-time All-Star, Howard is also the first African-American to play for the New York Yankees. He joined the club in 1955 but for years was used primarily in the outfield.

July 12
1966

St. Louis Cardinal's catcher **Tim McCarver** scores the winning run in the tenth inning of All Star game. In '66, McCarver bangs out thirteen triples for the season, nearly twice his career high in any other year. It is enough to lead the National League, the first time a catcher in either league has led in triples.

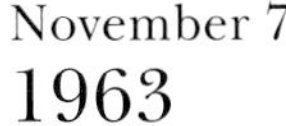

November 7
1963

August 22
1965

After complaining that Dodger catcher **John Roseboro's** throws back to pitcher Sandy Koufax are too close to his head, Giants pitcher Juan Marichal attacks Roseboro with his bat, setting off one of the worst brawls in major league history. Marichal is later fined a then-record $1,750. A four-time National League All-Star and two-time Gold Glove Award winner, Roseboro caught the first two of Koufax's four no-hitters, one in 1962 and one in 1963.

May 2
1970

The Philadelphia Phillies use three catchers—**Tim McCarver, Mike Ryan and Jim Hutto**—in a single inning when both McCarver and Ryan are forced to leave the game after suffering broken hands against the San Francisco Giants.

July 14
1970

In one of the most famous plays in All-Star game history, Pete Rose barrels over catcher **Ray Fosse** at the plate to score the winning run for the National League in the bottom of the twelfth inning. Fosse was the only catcher drafted ahead of Johnny Bench in the 1965 draft. In 1990 Pete Rose was convicted of tax evasion and sentenced to the federal penitentiary in Marion, Illinois, Ray Fosse's hometown.

November 22
1968

Johnny Bench is elected the National League's Rookie of the Year, the first catcher to win the award. Bench will go on to reinvent the position and will popularize such changes as wearing a helmet while catching and using a hinged catcher's mitt. The Johnny Bench Award for the best collegiate catcher was established in 2000.

July 14
1972

Both Bill and **Tom Haller** are behind the plate. Bill is the umpire, and Tom is the catcher, the first brother umpire-catcher combination in major league history.

October 22
1972

Oakland A's **Gene Tenace** is the first catcher in history to be named the World Series MVP as his team triumphs over the Reds. In 1976, Reds catcher Johnny Bench wins the award.

October 21
1975

In the twelfth inning, Red Sox catcher **Carlton Fisk** hits a 1-0 pitch down the left field line and above the Green Monster for a 7-6 victory over the Cincinnati Reds to send the World Series to a seventh game. It is the final play in what many consider to be the greatest World Series game ever.

November 21
1972

Future Hall of Famer **Carlton Fisk** is the first unanimous selection as American League Rookie of the Year.

August 2
1979

New York Yankee catcher **Thurman Munson** dies in a plane crash while practicing landings in Canton, Ohio.

Baltimore's **Rick Dempsey** is the third catcher in as many years to at least share the World Series MVP Award. Darrell Porter of the St. Louis Cardinals won it in 1982 and Steve Yeager of the Los Angeles Dodgers shared the award in 1981 with teammates Ron Cey and Pedro Guerrero.

October 16
1983

August 9
1981

Montreal backstop and future Hall of Famer **Gary Carter** bangs two home runs on his way to becoming the first catcher in history to be named Most Valuable Player of the All-Star Game. He would win the award again in 1984. The honor is also won by Terry Steinbach in 1988, Mike Piazza in 1996, and Sandy Alomar Jr. in 1997.

January 9
1989

Former National League Rookie of the Year, fourteen-time All-Star selection, ten-time Gold Glove Award winner and two-time National League MVP **Johnny Bench** is elected to the Baseball Hall of Fame on the first ballot. He receives more than 96 percent of the vote, the third highest percentage in history behind Ty Cobb and Hank Aaron.

May 9
1984

Carlton Fisk catches a 25-inning game, the longest ever by a major league catcher.

July 28
1991

Montreal Expos catcher **Ron Hassey** catches his second perfect game. The first was thrown by Cleveland's Len Barker, a 3-0 win over Toronto on May 15, 1981. Dennis Martinez throws the second against Los Angeles. Hassey is the only catcher in history to catch two perfect games in the major leagues.

May 13
1997

Catcher **Charlie O'Brien** of the Toronto Blue Jays is the first to wear the modified catcher's mask reminiscent of a hockey goalie's mask. The new type has since become the standard mask, offering both protection and visibility.

2002

The Phillies' **Mike Lieberthal** is the first catcher to win the Comeback Player of the Year award. Coincidentally, in 1997 Lieberthal replaced the team's stalwart backstop Darren Daulton, who was moved to right field and then dealt to the Florida Marlins, where he continued to play the outfield and won the Comeback Player of the Year. In 2003, the award again will be won by a catcher—Atlanta's Javy Lopez.

May 4

2004

Mike Piazza breaks Carlton Fisk's career home run record for catchers by belting number 352. By the end of the season, Piazza had 358 homers as a catcher.

2004

Cardinals catcher **Mike Matheny** sets three records in a single season, which could be a record in itself:
Most consecutive errorless games in a season—138
Most consecutive errorless games in a career—252
Most consecutive errorless chances in a career—1,555

4TH

A Day in the Life of a Catcher—Charles Johnson

On the afternoon of August 16, 2003 the visiting clubhouse at Shea Stadium looks pretty much like it always does on game day. Open lockers, loosely ordered by player uniform number, wrap around all four walls. Three televisions sit atop shelves installed on a center column. Underneath one is a VCR. Underneath another is a white-topped table with neatly stacked envelopes and tickets so players can leave passes for family and friends. Just out from the third television, farthest away from the clubhouse entrance, is another white-topped table where relief pitchers play cards.

The team bus is early—4:30 for a 7:10 game—because traffic from the Colorado Rockies' midtown Manhattan hotel to Shea is lighter today, a Saturday, than it would be during the week. One of the Rockies who exits the bus is catcher Charles Johnson. His family calls him Darius or Bump. Sometimes his wife calls him Charles. Everyone else calls him CJ.

Tonight CJ will catch his 1126th major league game. He is in his tenth major league season, his first with the Rockies. Johnson played on the 1992 Olympic team, is a two-time National League All-Star, has caught every no-hitter (three) thrown in Florida Marlins history, and owns more National League Gold Glove awards (four) than any catcher this side of Johnny Bench.

But the Rockies have lost five of their last six contests, including Wednesday night's game in Montreal that was delayed for an hour and fourteen minutes by a power outage at Olympic Stadium, and they have the worst road record of any team in the National League. On their only off-day during this roadtrip, the Rockies are in New York to experience firsthand the biggest blackout in United States history.

At 4:10 PM on Thursday, August 14, 2003, Charles Johnson was shopping with his wife, Rhonda, at Dr. J's, a clothing store across the street from the Empire State Building. It took his driver almost two hours to make it back to the team's hotel eight blocks away. Power had yet to be restored when the team left Friday afternoon for that night's game, which meant the only food available at the team's hotel was turkey sandwiches and chips. The water in the showers was cold. So were the Rockies. They lost that night to the Mets 5-0, and what hope they had for a possible wildcard playoff berth at the beginning of this six-game roadtrip was effectively extinguished.

* * * * *

Karan Rinaldo

CHARLES JOHNSON

Saturday morning, with power restored, Charles Johnson wakes up at 9:30, a relatively late hour for the father of two boys, five and two. He showers, dresses, goes downstairs for coffee and breakfast, visits nearby shops with his wife, comes back to the hotel for a turkey sandwich and a power nap before heading to the ballpark.

To say that 2003 has been a disappointing year for the New York Mets would be an understatement. They've fired their general manager. Starter Pedro Astacio, earn-ing seven million dollars this year, made just seven appearances with an ERA of over seven before having season-ending surgery on June 11. Set-up man Scott Strickland had season-ending surgery for a pulled groin four days earlier. First baseman Mo Vaughn played just twenty-seven games and batted less than .200 before calling it quits on his seventeen-million-dollar season. In mid-May, Mike Piazza—the Mets' best hitter, most popular player and ten-time All-Star—went down with a groin injury that ate three months of his season. Before the July 31 trading deadline the Mets dumped starting right-fielder Jeromy Burnitz, closer Armando Benitez, shortstop Rey Sanchez, and twelve-time All-Star second baseman Roberto Alomar. Their most highly touted off-season acquisition, former Atlanta Braves pitcher Tom Glavine, has a losing record and an ERA of nearly five.

But the Mets, perhaps owing to the psychological effects of Piazza's return from the disabled list on Wednesday, are clicking on all remaining cylinders. They've won seven of their last ten games, including the first three of their current homestand, two against the San Francisco Giants and Friday night's combined four-hit shutout of the Rockies by Glavine, Mike Stanton, and Grant Roberts.

Starters Glavine, Al Leiter, and Steve Trachsel are pitching well, and rookie Aaron Heilman picked up his second major league win and his first at Shea on Tuesday night, despite having an ERA of close to seven and a half. Outfielder Roger Cedeño is swinging the bat as well as he has since rejoining the Mets in 2002, flirting with a .400 batting average for the month of August. Piazza went three for five with a home run and five RBI in his first game back (which just happened to be "Italian Night" at the stadium), and rookie Jose Reyes has a fourteen-game hitting streak.

The Mets' front office sees rain in the forecast for Saturday night's game, and though the skies do not at all appear threatening, both teams take batting practice in the cages underneath Shea's right field stands. After the Rockies conduct a team stretch inside the visiting clubhouse, Johnson sits with pitching coach and former Met Bob Apodaca and tonight's starter, Shawn Chacon, in front of the pitcher's locker to discuss strategies for pitching to the Mets' lineup.

Mike Piazza has come to bat ten times against Shawn Chacon in his career and has two walks and three hits, two of them homers.

"I've got a good idea about what we're going to do with Piazza," CJ says. "His timing's not back yet probably, but he's going to get there. He's still dangerous. He's one of those guys that's still dangerous if you put a bat in his hand. Him and Cliff Floyd are the guys you really don't want to beat you. You'll probably let anybody beat you but Piazza.

"Normally he covers the outside pitch very well. Most guys try to pound him in, because when he's going well he doesn't pull the ball. But right now his timing's off so he's pulling everything.

"He's the guy that I don't want to beat us. I don't want the game to be over and say, Wow, we let Piazza beat us. You really can't do that. It happens sometimes. Sometimes you try to make pitches and you hang them. You might try to throw the curveball in the dirt, but he hangs it and the hitter hits a homerun. He might try to throw a fastball inside off the plate but he misses. The game is about inches. If you don't make your pitches on these guys, they capitalize."

At 6:40, Johnson grabs his catching gear and joins Chacon, backup catcher Mandy Romero, and reserve infielder Greg Norton in left field to loosen up with a session of long toss. Chacon and Romero exit first to the visitor's bullpen just steps away behind the left field fence while Johnson puts on his shinguards and begins a series of long stretches—butterfly stretches, hurdler stretches, lunge stretches—a man alone in the outfield as the stands begin to fill with patrons. Johnson gets on his knees, arches his back toward the bullpen, then reverses direction. He slowly twists side-to-side. The catcher stands 6'3" tall and weighs 250 pounds but bends with yoga precision.

Finally he pulls the chest protector over his head, returns his flapless catcher's helmet to his head and jogs slowly to the bullpen gate to replace Romero in warming up his pitcher. Not all major league catchers spend time in the bullpen before the game. Whether or not they do generally comes down to personal preference.

Jason Kendall does not. Mike Piazza does not. CJ takes pre-game throws from his pitcher because he likes going to the bullpen, "seeing what he's got down there before the game."

Though one would believe that throwing warm up to the catcher who will catch him during the game would help the pitcher, Johnson says, "I do it for me mostly, to give me an idea of what he's throwing, how he's looking. Plus, it helps me get my body going, get my body loose."

The game begins at 7:10. The game-time temperature is seventy-eight degrees, and the forecast rain that compelled the teams to take batting practice inside fails to materialize. The Rockies manage one run on two hits against starting pitcher Jae Weong Seo in the first inning, which concludes with Larry Walker striking out.

Shawn Chacon, tonight's starting pitcher for the Rockies, takes the hill. The twenty-five-year-old right-hander is making his twenty-third start of the season, his third in the major leagues. He's listed as 6'3", 210 pounds, but he's shorter than the 6'3" Johnson. Chacon set a Rockies record by winning eleven games before the All-Star break this year, and he was selected to the team, but he hasn't won since. He was put on the disabled list with right elbow inflammation on July first and watched the game from the bench. This will be his sixth start since coming off the DL.

The Rockies wear purple jerseys, gray pants with purple pinstripes, and black hats with a purple CR trimmed in silver. Chacon's hat, rather than facing straight ahead, is angled slightly toward the left.

"He says he's always done that," CJ says. "It looks straight to him, but it's not."

The Rockies' lead doesn't last long.

Johnson sets up outside for the first pitch to left-handed-batting outfielder Roger Cedeño in the bottom of the first, but Chacon's offering sails low and inside for a ball. Call it foreshadowing. Chacon's second pitch goes to the same place, which gives Cedeño a 2-0 advantage in the count. Johnson once again sets up on the outside corner and Cedeño promptly lines Chacon's pitch into right centerfield for a stand-up double.

Jose Reyes, a switch-hitter batting left against Chacon, grounds hard to second base, and though Ronnie Belliard of the Rockies looks to third as Cedeño advances, he flips to first for the easy out. This brings up Piazza with a man on third base and only one out. CJ wants to pound Piazza inside, but sets up away, a target Chacon hits, for ball one. A high and inside pitch to Piazza is fouled back to even the count. Chacon's third pitch, a fastball low but down the middle of the plate, is hit right back through the box and fielded by Belliard behind second base but not in time to throw out either Cedeño who crosses home for the Mets' first run, or Piazza hustling to first.

CJ is quiet, soft-spoken, reserved. Cliff Floyd, his friend and the next batter up, is not. Floyd shows his broad smile frequently. The pair were teammates on the Florida Marlins the previous year. They both live in south Florida in the off-season, less than five miles apart, and often work out together. Floyd, during those car rides to the gym, often threatens to steal a base on CJ, who possesses one of the strongest and most accurate arms in the major leagues, having thrown out more than forty percent of attempting base stealers over his career. Last night, after getting hit by a pitch in the fourth inning, Floyd ran on the next pitch even though he will shut his season down two days from now for surgery on an Achilles heel that has troubled him all season long. Johnson's throw sailed into centerfield and allowed Floyd to take third base on Johnson's third error of the season. CJ is expecting a comment.

"That mask makes you look even darker," Floyd says as he steps into the batter's box. Chacon walks Floyd on four pitches. The last pitch is outside, not even close to the strike zone.

Rookie Jason Phillips, thrown into the role of everyday starter with the injuries to Vaughn at first and Piazza behind the plate, comes up next, and CJ goes to the mound for a visit. Chacon has struggled thus far, and CJ's visit is a bid to buy time for Chacon to step back, relax, focus, gain his composure.

The first two pitches to Phillips, like the first two pitches to Cedeño to lead off the game, are outside and off of the plate. Chacon's third pitch to Phillips is a strike down the middle, and with his recent wildness, seems to surprise the batter. He doesn't see another good one. Chacon's 2-1 pitch is a slider outside. The next pitch, Johnson says, "was supposed to be a fastball inside. I've never seen anything like it before in my life. It was a fastball and he threw it, and it almost hit the grass. It scared me because when it's that far out, you can't really block it. You try not to get hurt. You really hope it doesn't hit you."

The errant pitch hits the backstop wall so hard that the ensuing bounce back to Johnson doesn't allow the runners a chance to advance. But the bases are now loaded, and Chacon has walked the previous two batters with pitches that weren't even close.

Pitching coach Bob Apodaca decides it's time to visit with Chacon, and CJ joins them on the mound. Apodaca wants Chacon to throw directly to CJ, meaning that he, like Johnson, has noticed that Chacon's shoulder is pulling off, or opening up, during his delivery. The meeting is quick. Chacon merely nods, spits, says "Okay," and maintains an understandable visage of frustration as outfielder Timo Perez approaches the batter's box.

Chacon throws a seventy-two-mile-an-hour curve high and inside to the left-hander for ball one, a seventy-eight-mile-an-hour change-up high and outside for ball two and the fifth 2-0 count of this, the first inning. And every one of the previous batters to receive a 2-0 count has either scored or is now on base. Perez sits on the eighty-nine-mile-an-hour fastball, a good low pitch, and slams it into deep center field where it is caught short of the warning track by center fielder Preston Wilson.

Piazza tags up from third and scores. Floyd moves up to third.

CJ says, "It was a great pitch. It was a two-seamer down in the zone, but Timo, he probably saw on-deck, he really wasn't throwing a whole lot of strikes, so in that situation you're dead red. I mean, he was dead red. He got him 2 and 0. He knew he was coming in there. Sometimes it can be a good pitch, but if you know it's a fastball you can probably hit it."

Ty Wigginton, the Mets' third baseman, is now up with two outs and Chacon goes low and away with a slider for ball one. The 1-0 pitch is a ninety-mile-an-hour fastball down the middle, and Wigginton pulls it to the warning track, where left-fielder Jay Payton is waiting, for the third out. Wigginton's swing is a close call. He was sitting on the fastball, and Johnson says, "just missed it." If he hadn't gotten underneath the ball by just a bit, the score after the first inning, could easily be 5-1 instead 2-1 Mets.

In the Rockies' dugout Charles Johnson removes his catcher's gear and grabs a bat—thirty-four-and-a-half inches long and thirty-three ounces in weight—and prepares to move on-deck as he's due up third in the bottom of the second.

Colorado manager Clint Hurdle approaches Chacon and asks if he's injured. Hurdle points out that when a pitcher is injured, the first thing to go is command, something Chacon has yet to acquire in tonight's game. Chacon denies being hurt.

A step off the on-deck circle, CJ stretches the bat high above his head, perpendicular to his body, one hand on either end. He brings the bat down, wipes his brow with his right shirt sleeve, shakes the white weighted donut down the shaft of the bat and comes to the plate with Jay Payton on third and one man out.

In the box, Johnson brushes the dirt from right to left with his right foot. He assumes a classic stance, as if he had learned the art from his father, a high school baseball coach at Fort Pierce Westwood in Florida, where Charles played ball and was selected Gatorade Player of the Year his senior season. His back arm is raised almost above his shoulder. The bat, kept in motion by a consistent arm movement, moves in a halo above his head.

"I'm trying to get some timing going," CJ says. "Sometimes I have a tendency to hit from a standstill, and it kind of goes against me a little bit. I try to get a little rhythm to get it going."

Johnson's best season as a hitter came in 2000, when he hit .304 with thirty-one home runs and ninety-one RBIs playing in a total of 128 games with the Baltimore Orioles and Chicago White Sox. The average fell nearly fifty points and home runs dropped almost in half the following year, but the injury-plagued 2002 season was a disaster. Held to just eighty-three games, his lowest total since making the majors, Johnson batted a woeful .217 with only six homeruns for the Florida Marlins before being traded to the Rockies.

Detractors say Johnson's swing is longer, that he's not the contact hitter he once was, and coming into tonight's game he is batting a mere .236, though he has hit a respectable fifteen homeruns and has fifty-two RBIs. (He will finish the year at .230.) Worse yet is his team-mirroring home vs. road batting average—over .300 at home, under .165 on the road.

Johnson is known for taking the first pitch—"Sometimes I like to see a pitch to get my timing," he says—and perhaps no statistic is as supportive of that fact as Johnson's 2003 batting average on an 0-1 count. Since the batter is generally considered to be "in the hole" when the count is against him, it might be a reasonable assumption to expect that Johnson hits as much as fifty points lower from the 0-1 count. Instead, through CJ's first eighty-seven games of the year, he is actually batting over .500 when the count is 0-1.

Seo's first pitch is a low-and-outside slider for called strike one by umpire Tim McClelland. A ninety-mile-an-hour fastball is outside to bring the count to 1-1. An eighty-one-mile-an-hour change-up is outside again for a 2-1 count.

"Early on I was looking for something more inside," CJ says. "I thought he would try to pound me early because of Payton on third base."

Seo never does throw Johnson an inside pitch. After working the pitcher to a full count, Johnson bounces a ball to deep third. Payton breaks on the pitch and is caught in an abbreviated rundown—third to catcher to third. Johnson is stranded at first when Chacon grounds out to end the inning.

Joe McEwing leads off the bottom of the second for the Mets with a walk. Pitcher Jae Weong Seo bunts him to second before Roger Cedeño walks, Chacon's third walk of the evening. Jose Reyes, the hot rookie shortstop, laces a double down the left-field line. McEwing scores from second and Cedeño safely slides headfirst into third.

Chacon has faced eleven batters and managed to throw just two first pitch strikes. Piazza is batting .500 with six RBI in ten at-bats since coming off the disabled list, and CJ looks into the dugout and sees four fingers held up so he stands to accept four intentionally wide pitches from Chacon, bringing up Cliff Floyd with the bases loaded and only one out.

"Floyd's a big guy," CJ says. "He's got a long reach. Anybody with a long reach like that, most of the time you want to pound them inside. Most of the time you can get him inside, but you have to get it in there. I mean, you can't miss the inner third or inside corner because he's so far off the plate that inside corner to him could be almost down the middle, so you have to really get it off the plate."

Chacon muscles up and throws his fastest pitch of the night, ninety-one miles an hour, as if he realizes this at-bat, even in the second inning, could effectively end the night for himself and his team, and Floyd fouls the pitch back for strike one. Another ninety-one-mile-an- hour fastball misses inside to even the count, and then a third fastball—since it seems this is the only pitch that Chacon has a chance of throwing for a strike—is strong and low across the plate, sawing off Floyd's bat in the process. But he is able to muscle it to the edge of the outfield grass in right, scoring two more runs as Piazza takes third.

"Great pitch to a guy that's big and strong, and he muscled it out," CJ says. "Maybe a smaller guy the ball wouldn't have went as far."

First baseman Jason Phillips approaches the plate for the second time this evening, and for the second time tonight pitching coach Bob Apodaca comes out of the dugout to talk to Chacon on the mound. CJ meets him there. Jose Jimenez, who started the year as the Rockies' closer, begins to warm up in the bullpen. The Mets lead by four with runners on first and third in the bottom of the second inning and there's still only one out.

Phillips punches a rare curve, moving low and away on a 2-2 count, into center field, scoring Piazza to increase the lead to five. Rockies' manager Clint Hurdle comes out to take the ball from Chacon, ending what will be his shortest and last outing of the season.

Jimenez comes in from the bullpen. He is a 6'3" 230-pound right-hander who lost his job as the closer to Josh Speier in light of Jimenez's ERA of nearly six. His frame and throwing motion yields an impression of gangliness, especially toward the end of his delivery when, for a split second, it appears that his whole body is motionless save for his right arm. In fact, it appears as if Jimenez might be trying to throw his arm off.

Despite his size, Jimenez is not a typical closer. He began his career as a starter, and throws a fastball in the low nineties on top of a slider. He has never developed an off-speed pitch. While it is not surprising that a closer would have only two pitches, the fact that his fastball tops out in the low nineties (rather than a higher speed) *is* surprising.

Jimenez's first pitch, an eighty-eight-mile-an-hour fastball, to Timo Perez is thrown to almost the exact spot as Chacon's 2-0 pitch to Perez, a hard hit ball that ended up in the glove of Preston Wilson in center for a sacrifice fly. This low fastball, however, is hit to Wilson's left and finds the alley between center and right before bouncing off the wall between Wilson and Larry Walker. The hit scores two and Perez settles into second.

Jimenez manages to get Ty Wigginton to ground out to second, Joe McEwing to ground out to third, but the damage is done as the Mets lead the Rockies 8-1 after two innings.

In the top of the third inning, Rockies' second baseman Ronnie Belliard fouls a ball off his foot and into fair territory. The Mets field the ball and throw to first where Belliard, hobbling near home plate, bat still in hand, is called out. Manager Clint Hurdle comes out of the dugout to argue the call with Tim McClelland but the play stands.

Johnson brushes the dirt in front of the catcher's box, his work station, effectively wiping out what little is left of the back line of the batter's box. Back and forth, with both feet, back and forth, like a teenage boy trying to make his new sneakers look un-new. Back and forth, back and forth, until the line is completely gone.

Pitcher Jae Weong Seo leads off for the Mets in the bottom of the third, and Johnson and Jimenez waste no time. A fastball for strike one, a fastball grounded to short for out one. Cedeño follows and fails to check his swing on the outside corner. A low slider is swung on and missed. Jimenez's 0-2 pitch goes to where Johnson is set, off the outside corner, and the 1-2 pitch, a fastball, is grounded to second for the second out.

Jose Reyes is jammed on a slider thrown on a 1-1 count and weakly grounds to Jimenez for the 1-3 put out. The Mets are three up, three down on nine pitches. By contrast, Chacon threw fifty-two pitches in an inning and a third.

In the top of the fourth Larry Walker hits a ball 435 feet over the right-centerfield wall to close the gap to 8-2, but Garrett Atkins grounds out to third for the final out of the inning, leaving CJ in the on-deck circle so manager Clint Hurdle comes out to warm up Jimenez while Johnson dons shinguards, chest protector and mask. Jimenez throws three pitches to Johnson after Hurdle departs, and Johnson returns the ball to Jimenez who drops his hands, looks to second base, then turns back to Johnson as if to say, Do you want me to throw it to second? Instead, he throws one more warm-up to his catcher, who throws down to second to signal the battery's readiness.

Piazza leads off and fouls a fastball weakly back toward the first base dugout. From Piazza's swing, Johnson believes the ball is headed toward third base so he rises from his crouch and takes a step left. No one in the infield yells to correct him, and by the time he turns back to the right, the direction the ball has been hit, it lands harmlessly on the ground.

"It was a catchable ball," CJ says. "If I had seen it right away, I would've caught it. But I looked this way and I didn't see it. Once I look this way, I'm not going to look back. Usually you kind of look back this way, but by the time I did it was too late."

He gathers his mask, bangs it against his thigh to remove the dirt and settles back behind the plate. Piazza and McClelland, the umpire, say nothing. Piazza bloops the 0-1 pitch into short center where it is caught on an excellent play by Belliard.

Cliff Floyd takes a slider well off the plate, then golfs a low-and-away, ninety-one-mile-an-hour fastball into left for another single. Between batters, CJ goes down on his knees. He sets in a higher crouch with Floyd on first in preparation to throw, and first baseman Jason Phillips takes ball one low and away. CJ looks into the dugout for a possible pitch out, then sets up outside again. Phillips goes with the pitch, a low-and-away ninety-two-mile-an-hour fastball, depositing it into the rightfield corner. Second baseman Belliard takes the throw from Walker but CJ, realizing there will be no play on Floyd at home, blocks the relay throw in front of the plate, and Phillips stops at second with an RBI double.

Timo Perez grounds out to second, and Phillips moves to third. With Ty Wigginton up, CJ sits low, then comes up into his high crouch with Phillips on third, even though there will no attempted steal. He stays in that position with each pitch, and Wigginton weakly grounds a 2-1 slider to third, and the inning is over. The Mets lead the Rockies 9-2 after four.

CJ leads off the top half of the fifth after returning to the dugout to remove his chest protector and shin-guards. He brushes at the batter's box dirt with his feet, and digs in with his back foot. The top of the bat wiggles high above his head, and he hits the first pitch, a ninety-one-mile-an-hour fastball, to Roger Cedeño, short of the warning track, in right field.

"I thought I should've hit it better but I got under it," CJ says. "If I'd have got on top of it a little more I probably would've hit it a little better."

Seven runs down and the game less than halfway over, manager Clint Hurdle sends Jimenez to bat for himself and the reliever singles to left. After Tony Womack fouls out to first, Ronnie Belliard triples to deep right center, scoring Jimenez with the Rockies' third run. If Jimenez wasn't tired before, he is now. Belliard, a fast runner, nearly catches him between second and third.

Todd Helton, the Rockies' first basemen and one of the league's best hitters, lines to the right of the 410 marker in centerfield. The ball one-hops the fence, scoring Belliard, and Helton easily makes second with his one-hundredth RBI of the season, his fifth straight of one hundred RBI or more. A pinch-runner is called for. Mets' pitching coach Vern Ruhle calls to the bullpen to get someone warm. With his gear on CJ stands next to the water cooler in the dugout, where he remains as Preston Wilson flies out to end the inning.

Jimenez pitches to Joe McEwing, alternating balls with foul pitches, until McEwing softly lines the 2-2 offering to Greg Norton, who has replaced Helton at first base.

Veteran infielder Jay Bell, who once set a record for sacrifice bunts in a season while playing with Pittsburgh, pinch-hits for Jay Seo. CJ calls for a slow, looping curve from Jimenez that surprises Bell for strike one. The second pitch is an inside fastball that Bell fouls in the dirt. The third pitch is the same as the second—ninety-one-mile-an-hour fastball—but this time Bell takes the pitch. After two inside fastballs, CJ sets up outside and calls for another breaking pitch.

"I threw the curveball to Bell because he was coming off the bench," he says. "I was thinking he might be looking for a first-pitch fastball inside. And I threw the slider to keep him off-balance."

Bell works the count to 3 and 2 before hitting a low-and-away fastball to Preston Wilson in center for the second out. Leadoff man Roger Cedeño is up next, and despite the empty bases, Jimenez continues to work from the stretch. Every pitch to the switch-hitter is hard, low and away. He fouls off two, takes two for balls before swinging and missing a final low and outside fastball for the third out of the inning, just the second time all evening the Mets have been retired in order.

Dan Wheeler relieves Seo for the top of the sixth and walks Larry Walker on five pitches before inducing groundouts from Jay Payton and Garrett Atkins that have advanced Walker to third. Once again CJ swings at the first pitch, an eighty-six-mile-an-hour slider outside for strike one, before grounding another slider to deep short. A faster runner might make the play close, but CJ's lack of speed removes all drama before he is out of the batter's box.

The Mets lead 9-4 after five and a half. Jose Reyes leads off the bottom of the sixth. His stance appears malleable, spread but not open, farther up in the batter's box than most, and CJ still doesn't have a feel for how to pitch him.

"We tried to go down and away on him a few

times," he says, "but then I tried to come in on him late and he hit a ball to right-center. He seems to be a pretty good hitter. It's kind of weird. He kind of slaps it. I'm still trying to figure him out."

Inside breaking pitches and fastballs farther in bring the count to 2-2 before a high-and-outside fastball brings the count full. Another fastball on the payoff pitch is grounded in the dirt toward third and fielded by Jimenez who throws to third but is late. Reyes' speed garners a base hit.

Despite being down five runs in the bottom of the sixth inning, the Rockies act as if they're still in the ballgame. Mike Piazza is at the plate, and CJ looks into the Rockies' dugout to check the signs in case Reyes decides to run.

"I think we kind of have an idea of when it's appropriate to run or not," CJ says. "I don't think we think the game is ever over, but we know it's a tough battle to get back. Piazza comes in then, and I wasn't too sure if he [Reyes] was going or not. That's why I looked over for the sign. I felt like it was because if we're behind four or five runs I believe we still have a legitimate shot. Anything can happen, you know. But right there, with a big inning right then it could've killed our chances of trying to come back."

After ball one outside, CJ looks again into the dugout and rises to a ready throwing position. Norton holds Reyes on first, and Jimenez throws over. The next pitch to Piazza is a fastball, as good a pitch as

Piazza will see all evening, but he fouls it straight back into the upper deck. He grimaces with the knowledge that that was his pitch to hit. CJ stands out of his crouch, looks once more into the Rockies' dugout for a possible sign.

The 1-1 pitch is a slider well outside. Piazza takes. Then Jimenez tosses to first. And again. CJ sets inside but the pitch is a low and outside that forces Johnson to his knees as he catches the pitch in the dirt with his glove palm up. He scoots back behind the plate in a knees-only, lobster-esque shuffle.

Piazza reaches early for the 3-1 pitch outside and pulls it foul into the left field seats to bring the count full. After missing the 1-0 pitch he is anxious. Reyes maintains a lead at first, Johnson looks once more into the dugout. Jimenez comes out of his set position and looks to first. Fans half-heartedly yell, "Balk!"

Reyes goes on the pitch, an outside change-up that Piazza is once again early on, and he grounds weakly to shortstop. Clint Hurdle comes out of the dugout, motions to the bullpen, and meets Jimenez and CJ and shortstop Tony Womack on the mound. Hurdle says, "Good job," to Jimenez. Womack and CJ both touch the pitcher lightly, with gloved hands, on the shoulder before he walks to the dugout, then Hurdle exits after handing the ball to Javy Lopez.

Left-hander Lopez possesses one of the most awkward throwing motions in the major leagues. A submariner, his lanky build contributes to the feeling he is standing on two different sized step ladders in his set position. The motion is not only confusing for the hitters but for the catcher as well.

"It's tough," says CJ, "because he comes from an angle where you're not used to seeing it, so it takes a lot to track the ball."

As Cliff Floyd steps into the batter's box, CJ calls time and lets middle infielders know he'll call where the throw should be made in the event of a ground ball. CJ's preparation pays off as Floyd grounds a fastball to first for the second out, Norton's only play, as Reyes moves to third.

The dugout makes the decision to walk right-handed hitter Jason Phillips with two outs to bring up Timo Perez. Two successive sliders make Perez look awkward and overmatched, but an 0-2 belt-high fastball is lifted gently over third base, bringing home Reyes.

"He put it in the wrong place," CJ says. "We threw him two sliders, and he fouled the first one off, and then he fouled the next one off, but in my mind it looked like he was trying to hit the ball outside, so I didn't want to give him one more shot. So I thought we should show him an inside fastball off the plate to give him something to think about. Now he doesn't know whether I'm coming with another fastball in or a breaking ball away. I thought a fastball in, but he never did get it in there. He was supposed to go in, off for a ball, but he never did get it there."

A 1-0 slider to the right-handed Ty Wigginton

bounces in the dirt at his feet and gets by CJ. Phillips moves to third and Perez to second, and so with two outs, Lopez throws two more balls wide of the plate to intentionally walk the Mets' third baseman. Lopez's second pitch to Joe McEwing, a mid-eighties fastball down the middle, is ground sharply to third and Wigginton is forced at second for the final out of the inning.

CJ greets a new pitcher, Adam Bernero, on the mound. Bernero is a recent acquisition from the Detroit Tigers, and CJ has only caught him a couple of times in game situations. The reliever gets two swinging strikes on a couple of fastballs to pinch-hitter Raul Gonzalez, then throws another fastball to the outside corner where CJ is set for a ball. CJ calls for another fastball away, but Bernero shakes him off to the split-finger, "the splitty" CJ calls it, which Gonzalez chases for strike three.

Outfielder Roger Cedeño stands in the box to begin as interesting an at-bat as can be conceived in a 10-4 ballgame. Bernero throws a ninety-two-mile-an-hour fastball for a called first strike, but the ball hits off of CJ's glove and bounces away. Umpire Tim McClelland assumes the ball was a foul tip off Cedeño's bat. McClelland asks Cedeño if he tipped it and Cedeño says no.

"The ball," CJ says, "when I was getting ready to receive it, cut a little bit. At the last minute it cut, and I tried to frame it because it was a pitch down and away, and I missed it. Tim thought that he fouled it. I didn't think he fouled it. It nicked my glove and sounded like he fouled it. Cedeño was telling him, 'I didn't foul it.' But Tim was saying, 'You fouled it.'"

Cedeño and McClelland continue their discussion in good humor. It is, after all, a six-run ballgame. Bernero's second pitch, a splitter, bounces in the dirt away from CJ who is 0 for 2 catching pitches this at-bat, but it's a 1-1 count on Cedeño.

The 2-2 pitch to Cedeño is lined right back to the box where it catches Bernero squarely on the jaw. Coaches run from the dugout, McClelland goes out, and the entire Colorado infield, minus CJ, gathers on the mound around the fallen pitcher.

"I didn't go out there, you know," CJ says. "I really didn't want to see what happened. I kind of hate seeing that. I knew it hit him up here in the neck area."

There's no blood. Bernero shakes his head from side to side and remains in the game, though he will hold an ice pack to the side of his face for most of the next two days.

Jose Reyes lines Bernero's third pitch to right field for a double, and Cedeño moves to third. CJ looks to the bench to see if they want to intentionally walk Piazza, but no sign is given, as sure a symbol as any that this game, at least in the minds of the coaching staff, is already lost.

Piazza takes the first two pitches outside, swings awkwardly at a 2-0 change outside again, before taking a massive cut at what can only be called a mystery pitch that sails high and inside toward Piazza's head.

"It was a slider," CJ says. "It backed up. Piazza was upset. It was a terrible pitch because it backed up, and he swung at it. I think he was upset about that."

Piazza steps out of the batter's box in disgust. CJ stays set in his crouch behind the plate, and umpire McClelland puts his hand on CJ's shoulder.

"He was telling me to give Piazza time, because Piazza called time out. And he was telling me, 'Give him a little second.'"

Piazza takes ball four. Hurdle comes to the mound again to replace yet another pitcher. Both Hurdle and Johnson pat Bernero as he's relieved by Brian Fuentes, who will face Cliff Floyd with the bases loaded.

During warm-ups Fuentes holds his glove at the belt, and swings his body out wide toward first base with a sidearm, though overhand, motion. He holds up a finger to CJ, then stands on the third base side of the mound as the catcher throws down to second.

Cliff Floyd stands in back of the box, his front foot turned slightly inward, and pulls Fuentes' first pitch, a fastball up and in, to right field for a single. Cedeño scores from third, Reyes from second. CJ moves up the line in foul territory to receive the relay from Walker in right, but Walker's throw misses the cutoff man, gets by CJ and Piazza ends up on third and Floyd on second where he is lifted for a pinch-runner.

Jason Phillips grounds out but scores Piazza and

Timo Perez pops out to end the inning with a score of 13 to 4 in favor of the Mets. CJ sits on the dugout bench to remove his catcher's gear, then wipes his face with a white towel.

Justin Speier, who has replaced Jimenez as the Rockies' closer comes in for Colorado to pitch the bottom of the eighth. He's just getting in some work. Substitutions rule both the field and the bench. Everyone is ready for the night to be over. The inning passes quickly, if not easily.

"I had a feeling that he was going to call anything close and not squeeze that late in the ballgame," CJ says of the umpire McClelland. "But Speier was locating pretty good so it helped. I try to stay the same, but you think, Let's go ahead and finish this thing."

Speier bends toward the plate, as if he has trouble seeing the catcher's sign, before straightening, adopting a high and pointed leg kick as he delivers the ball. He throws a fastball, slider and split-finger, two of which bounce in the dirt for Johnson to block.

Ty Wigginton leads off. He doesn't know CJ but speaks to him briefly about the long evening before stepping in and striking out on an inside fastball. Joe McEwing takes a high-and-outside fastball for strike one and decides he better widen his zone. The second pitch, another fastball outside, is grounded weakly to third for the second out.

Raul Gonzalez works a full count before grounding back up the middle and off of Speier's glove for an infield hit before Tony Clark does everyone a favor by popping a slider to left for the final out.

But the night's not quite over. CJ has one more at-bat against reliever David Weathers. Leadoff batter Jay Payton singles to center, then Garrett Atkins lines out to left. CJ stands in, takes a fastball low and away for strike one, swings and badly misses a slider outside for strike two, and then calls time.

"It was 0-2," he says. I thought he kind of quick-pitched me a little bit and I called time out."

The 0-2 pitch is a fastball outside and CJ fouls the next pitch into the loge level on the first base side. A 1-2 fastball comes inside followed by a slider outside to bring the count full. With a nine-run lead, Weathers delivers a fastball that CJ fouls off his front foot and down the third base line. Weathers' second 3-2 pitch is hit loud and long, but not long enough as it's caught on the warning track in left.

"I just missed that ball," CJ says. "He tried to come inside on me, and I just missed it. Just a little bit on top, and I'd hit a home run."

Juan Uribe follows by grounding to second for the final out of the game.

The visiting clubhouse is open to the media ten minutes after the final pitch. Reporters race through the door and turn the corner to the manager's office to ask Clint Hurdle about the health of Shawn Chacon, Todd

Helton, and Adam Bernero. They ask about the team's motivation, the unsuccessful road trip then leave for Chacon's locker where the pitcher will give his last post-game interview of the season.

CJ's already showered and dressed in the corner of the room.

"It was a tough game," he says. "It was a long game, you know, because you couldn't really get nothing going. It seemed like Chacon was scuffling and then what happens is whenever your starter comes out early you catch a lot of guys. You change signs a lot. It makes the day longer. Every inning or so you got to see another guy come in. Plus," he says, "it was humid. It was hot."

CJ signs a few autographs on his way to the players' gate entrance to meet his wife and two of her cousins who have driven down from Connecticut for the game. They'll go into the city and get a bite to eat before calling it a night. He'll wake up on the thirty-third floor of a midtown Manhattan hotel room the following morning and go to work again.

5TH

What it Takes

Spend any time at all discussing traits necessary to become a successful catcher and you will hear the words "soft hands." More than likely you will hear the words "soft hands" within the first fifteen seconds of conversation. "Soft hands" comes up in conversation with such frequency that you can almost imagine a large, oversized hand—perhaps the spokeshand for Hamburger Helper, or maybe the oven mitt that shills on behalf of Arby's—attaining All-Star status if they could just find a uniform that would fit.

But what do players really mean when they say that a catcher needs "soft hands"? Bob Geren, bullpen coach for the Oakland A's, says that the hands are actually the final ingredient.

"It's really not just the hands," he says. "It's the whole upper body. It's a looseness to receiving the ball. Like a shortstop, just letting it come to them with their body relaxed, relaxed and not tense in going and getting balls. When they say it's your hands, that's really the last thing. It's your arms, your upper body, the muscles in your neck. You see some catchers back there that seem to be all tight. They just don't look comfortable. Usually if a guy has stiff hands, he has stiff actions all the way around, up and down. He doesn't look good anywhere. If a guy's real soft, everything's kind of soft."

Adam Melhuse, brought up by the A's in 2003 to back up Ramon Hernandez, is a converted catcher. He realizes that there are elements of the job—blocking balls in the dirt, footwork—that he occasionally struggles with, but he believes his years as an infielder served as a positive in developing "soft hands."

Melhuse's conversion from infielder to catcher, just one in a long line of so many other converted backstops, is a strong argument that catchers are made rather than born—and that "soft hands" can be developed.

Joe Ayrault, a former catcher with the Atlanta Braves, is currently the hitting coach for the Single A Stockton Ports. "The key to having soft hands is not closing the glove," he says, "but letting the ball close the glove for you. They used to have me working with a glove without a hinge, like the old-timer gloves. One of my first coaches, Joe Pignatano, always had me catch bullpen with a glove without a hinge in it, which was kind of wild. You'd have to use two hands. I started thinking about it. That's a key to having soft hands, just letting the ball close the glove for you."

Don Werner has been coaching in the minor leagues for several years. Call it a pet peeve or something more substantial, but Werner has issues with the way modern catchers receive the ball.

"There used to be an art form," Werner says, "to where you'd catch the ball out front and you'd have a little bit of drawback. The word 'receiving,' to me, means something. If we're going to work on our receiving, we're not going to go back there and work on our jerking or stabbing. We're going to work on receiving the ball. That word means you're lightly catching the ball. You're not bringing it back a lot. You're taking the pounding off your hand with that little bit of softness. That's what makes soft hands."

You don't have to spend much time with catchers to realize that "stab" is a bad word, an inflammatory word, little less than an accusation of bad catching.

"I'm not a stabber," Todd Greene says. Now in his mid-thirties, Greene has become a journeyman utility player, finishing 2004 with the Rockies, his fifth major league team. His 2003 season with Texas was the first he hadn't started a game in the outfield, though he managed starts at first, behind the plate, and as the Rangers' DH.

"I probably catch the ball as deep as any catcher in the big leagues," Greene says. "I'm not saying I'm the deepest, and I'm not saying that's a good thing. I'm saying that's the way I do it. There are a lot of stabbers. I think it looks bad, personally. The umpires don't want to see a catcher doing that kind of shit. They want to see you catch it and throw it back. That's not how I was taught, and I prefer not seeing it."

Greene mentions Terry Steinbach and Charlie O'Brien as strong defensive role models, catchers that he watched and studied.

"Charlie moved his hips and caught everything inside his body," Greene says. "Now if the ball's over here, and it's clearly a ball, yeah, I'll reach out and throw it back. But if it's a good pitch I'm going to let the ball travel and catch it as deep as I can and let that umpire see it as long as he can."

Don Werner completes the thought.

"That little bit of receiving skill where you're drawing it in just a couple of inches," he says. "Today I watch catchers and I'm trying to figure out where this all started, but you see guys almost acting like they're back in Little League, where the guys are jerking the ball back in the strike zone. If you did that when I played the umpire would say, 'What are you trying to do? You think I'm an idiot?' He'd kick you in the butt or something, where today I see big league guys doing it and I can't believe it.

"But I'm on a mission to find out where that started. I know every time I talk to an umpire I say, 'How do you call that ball a strike when he jerks that in like that? He's telling you it's a ball.' And they'll say, 'There's not supposed to be any outside influences that affect our call.' I say, 'If a catcher does that, he's telling you it's a ball and I would call it a ball.' I don't know where it started, but I'm going to find out one of these days."

Don Wakamatsu's major league career consisted of catching eighteen games with the Chicago White Sox in 1991. Knuckleballer and future pitching coach Charlie Hough was on the mound every time. Wakamatsu now serves as Buck Showalter's bench coach in Texas.

"Charlie and I had a good relationship in spring training," he says, "and I caught him one time, and then he asked for me to catch on the minor league side. Charlie very rarely made road trips, because he's not a guy they particularly needed to see during the course of spring training to make the club. They just needed him to get his work in. So Charlie would stay back, or pitch in the day game on the minor league side, and I would go over there and catch him. I ended up catching him five or six times, so we built a pretty good relationship. Then the opportunity happened where Carlton [Fisk] didn't want to catch him. I was hitting .190 at the time in Triple A, and Charlie said, 'I don't care what he's hitting. I want him to catch me.' I wouldn't have had any time in the big leagues at all if it wasn't for him requesting me."

Years as a minor league catcher, along with the experience of catching the knuckleball at the major league level, served as training for Wakamatsu to enter coaching.

"I was a roving catching instructor," Wakamatsu says. "There was a machine that came out a couple years ago that actually threw a knuckleball. We ended up using it in Anaheim. I loved using it with the younger kids because Charlie had said something to me that hit home. He said, 'I'll make you a better catcher.' I didn't understand at the time. I thought, 'Well, just because I have to catch the knuckleball.' But to catch the knuckleball you have to let the ball get to you. You can't reach out and catch it, and that applies to regular catching for me. You have to be patient enough to receive the ball. You don't stab at it.

"There's not another pitch, other than maybe a splitter or fork, that's even similar to it, that's that nasty. It just made you a more rounded catcher. I like young kids to catch the knuckleball. It will make them a better receiver. The hands have to be much softer."

Wakamatsu, however, is more forgiving than some of his counterparts in accepting different styles of receiving.

"There are different philosophies of catching," he says. "Some guys say, 'You've got to present the ball out in front of the plate so the umpire can see it.' Some guys say, 'No, you've got to funnel it into the middle of your chest.' Some guys say, 'You want to be quiet back there.' Some guys catch with a stiff arm. Some guys receive it closer to the body. Some guys do both. I think you've got to match it to the body type, the athleticism. You can't clone catching. There are different styles and there are successful styles throughout the history of catching.

"I was talking to one of our scouts and he asked, 'What do I look for in a good catcher?' We were talking about soft hands, but you can look at a catcher's glove and basically tell what type of catcher he is, or what style or what stance he uses, by the way he has to receive the baseball in the glove. Whether it's in one spot, he uses his whole glove, he uses a big mitt, a small mitt, keeps his finger out, puts his finger to the side. There are a lot of different styles that way.

"To me, when you talk about soft hands, everybody says, 'I want a catcher with soft hands, a catcher with good hands.' It's similar to watching a great shortstop. They don't actually squeeze to catch the baseball. They allow the ball to hit the mitt and their hand closes around it. That's how you get soft. It's like catching an egg. Some instructors, years ago, used to toss an egg just to get that feel."

But Wakamatsu agrees with Bob Geren—the hands are just one ingredient; the catcher's body must be loose.

"When you're catching a guy that's got good movement, you'll find that the more it moves the more we end up having to stab and squeeze to try to control the baseball. If there's a philosophy that I tried to instill in our catchers it would be to put your body in position to receive the ball soft. Some guys put themselves in a receiving stance that's so stagnant, that's so locked in, their glove will move first. You'll allow your body to be a lot more tension free if the stance is proper, if you're somehow getting your body in a position, whether it's outside or inside, to receive the ball in the middle.

"We can go on and on about umpires seeing the ball," Wakamatsu says, "too much movement, stabbing, jerking. It's more of an anticipation and a shift with the body, a quiet anticipated shift, to allow yourself to have soft hands. The more my glove gets out of the center of my body, the more strength it takes to control the baseball. So you'll see guys that receive the ball outside their body, which is—pounds per square inch, what have you—much, much harder to receive a baseball and keep it in the zone or make it presentable. Some guys will argue that's too much movement, but again if you watched Bob Boone, he did it like Houdini. He could move without the slightest hint of him actually jerking or moving his body in that position."

Obviously a catcher's body has as much to do with having "soft hands" as the hands themselves, so what's the ideal body type for a catcher?

The prototypical catchers body in the 1950s and 60s would stand between 5'10" and 6 feet tall and weigh between 180 and 200 pounds. Scouts looked for a fire-plug-type body—a certain stockiness for durability and, with hope, power. They wanted a shorter guy so he could stay low in the zone to give a target, receive pitches, and block errant throws. Todd Greene, at 5'10" and 195 pounds, fits perfectly but is much more muscular than the average backstop forty years ago.

Baseball players have gotten bigger over the years. Ivan Rodriguez is the smallest current major league catcher at a charitable 5'9". Meanwhile Sandy Alomar, Josh Bard, Ben Davis, Toby Hall, Charles Johnson, Javy

Lopez, Mike Matheny, Damian Miller, Chad Moeller, Mike Piazza, and A.J. Pierzynski are all listed at 6'3" or more, most likely representing either a broadening of views or an acquiescence to the offensive bias that has taken over the game.

Fran Healy played nine major league seasons at a lanky 6'5" and was on the receiving end of both no-hitters thrown by Steve Busby. Healy's uncle, Francis Healy, was a backup catcher with the New York Giants and St. Louis Cardinals in the early 1930s and played a significant role in his nephew's choice of position.

"My uncle was about 5'9" or 5'10"," Healy says. "My father was about 5'11" and I didn't realize I was going to be 6'5". If I had it to do over again I might've tried the mound because of my size and my arm.

"I think the shorter guy is able to get his body in position to throw better, quicker. The target I would give would be a little bit higher up than the pitcher would prefer. I never got down on my knee. I might be a little bit too tall to catch, although my prediction is that within this century we're going to see a seven-foot everyday player. Could be a shortstop, whatever. When I signed and went to spring training, I went to the major league camp when I was eighteen years old, and everybody came up to my shoulders. Now you go to a minor league camp, and I'm looking up. Players got bigger. So there will be catchers over 6' 5", I'm sure, before too long."

Flexibility is an important trait for all catchers, but even more essential for a player of height. "Everybody

IVAN RODRIGUEZ

talks about Pudge Rodriguez being small and low to the ground," Don Werner says, "and that's a big thing, but if you're built like Pudge and you don't have flexibility then you're not a catcher in my book. I look for flexibility, the number one thing."

Despite his relatively small size, when Todd Greene converted to the catcher position while in the Angels' minor league system, flexibility was an issue from the very beginning.

"I couldn't get down low enough," he says. "I couldn't find a comfortable position without killing my hip flexors and my knees. And that, in turn, made me uncomfortable as far as receiving the ball, catching the ball. That's the first thing you have to learn when you're becoming a catcher is catching the ball."

The ever-smiling Manny Sanguillen, a three-time All-Star overshadowed in the National League by his contemporary Johnny Bench, served as the Pittsburgh Pirates catcher for most of the 1970s. Sanguillen's receiving position was memorable, to say the least, as he adopted a splayed leg stance, giving the appearance of a lopsided spider, to give his pitchers a lower target.

Don Wakamatsu believes that it's not only the positioning behind the plate that must be considered with larger-bodied catchers, and uses long-time receivers

MANNY SANGUILLEN

Carlton Fisk and Sandy Alomar as examples.

"Usually the bigger they get," he says, "the more tendency you have toward back problems or knees. That's not a given, but a bigger man has to have extreme flexibility to endure that wear and tear, where maybe a smaller guy, it's not as devastating on his body. Whether there's truth to that or not, you notice it a little bit more. Carlton had a number of knee surgeries. Sandy's had some knee surgeries. Whatever position you play, flexibility plays a huge key, but especially catching."

One catching trait that is extremely important, but often overlooked due to its elementary nature, is, for lack of a better term, handedness. To be a major league catcher, you must be right handed.

Why are there no left-handed throwing catchers in the major leagues? For one thing, prejudice. The powers that be in baseball believe that a left-handed catcher would have more difficulty throwing out baserunners (a difficult task in itself) because the majority of batters are right-handed, thus impeding the catcher's throw to second and third base. But if you think about it, you almost never hear an announcer talk about a runner being more likely to steal second because a left-hander is at the plate, effectively blocking (to use old baseball logic) the right-handed catcher's throw.

By my count, no fewer than thirty-seven left-handed men have been behind the plate during a major league game; however, twenty-five of those men played before

1900. Since 1950, only four men have appeared behind the plate, and their combined career total of games caught is eight. This is not exactly a trend.

A more justifiable explanation of the paucity of left-handers becoming major league catchers does, however, have to do with arm strength. It's quite likely that a young left-hander with a strong arm would be steered away from catching and into pitching. Several left-handed relievers in recent years have been able to extend their playing careers well into their forties. Right-handed relievers in their forties are a much rarer item, and on this basis alone one might determine that left-handing pitching is a prized possession. So any left-hander with a strong enough arm to play catcher at the major league level will likely be given the opportunity to show his stuff on the mound first.

Benny Distefano, the last left-hander to catch in the big leagues, played five seasons in the majors over the years 1984-1992. He appeared in 240 games, but only in 124 games defensively. One might assume that Distefano's true position was pinch-hitter. He played seventy-seven games at first and forty-four games in the outfield. In his three games at catcher, all in 1989 with Pittsburgh, he had exactly two putouts, and so, given that the catcher is given credit for the putout on a strikeout, it would be safe to describe Benny Distefano as an emergency late-inning backstop.

The same can be said for Mike Squires, a ten-season major leaguer with the Chicago White Sox. Squires played in 688 games at first base, fourteen games at third, five in the outfield, five as the DH and even pitched an inning in 1984. Squires appeared in just two games at catcher and recorded one putout.

All-Star pitcher Chris Short played fourteen of his fifteen seasons with the Philadelphia Phillies, and in 1961 appeared in one game as catcher. In the first game of a doubleheader against the Giants on June 29th, 1961 Phillies manager Gene Mauch, attempting to hide his true starting pitcher, placed four hurlers—Don Lehman, Don Ferrarese, Jim Owens and Short—into his starting lineup. After two batters, Lehman was replaced by Dallas Green and Chris Short's catching career was over. The Phillies lost the game 8-7 in ten innings as Willie Mays hit three home runs, including the game winner.

Dale Long is the only other left-hander to catch in the majors after 1950. A ten-year veteran, Long played 819 games at first and one in the outfield besides two appearances behind the plate for the Cubs in 1958, including a ninth-inning appearance against the Dodgers in late September. The Cubs, facing Sandy Koufax, lost 2-1. Long's career catching statistics include zero putouts, but one assist and one passed ball.

In the course of a major league season, a starting catcher will receive somewhere in the neighborhood of 18,000 pitches. Figure 150 pitches a game for 120 games out of the 162 that comprise a regular season. So not counting amateur ball or spring training or warm-ups or bullpen activity, it should be a safe assumption that Ivan Rodriguez has adopted a catcher's squat nearly a quarter of a million times in his career.

No wonder back treatments and knee surgeries are often a part of the catcher's resume.

And yet, for all the physical demands that are placed on a catcher's body, it is the mental stress and strain that the majority of catchers find most exhausting. You've heard it said that the game can't start until the pitcher releases the ball. Well, the pitcher doesn't throw the ball until the catcher calls the pitch. He's not just flicking fingers at random back there. Before the catcher puts down the sign he's perused his team's defensive alignment to make certain it matches the way the team wants to defend the hitter now entering the batter's box. The catcher looks into the dugout to see if the bench coach has a play on, maybe a pitchout for the runner on first, or a wheel play in case of a bunt.

The catcher takes into consideration his pitcher's strengths and weaknesses. Not just what a scouting report might say, such as "good curve" or "nasty slider," but what's been effective for his pitcher that day. If his pitcher hasn't been able to throw a breaking ball for a strike and the batter has a disciplined zone, there's not much sense in calling for the curveball. Is he tired early? Is his fastball coming in flat? Without any movement? Where's his head? The release point in his delivery? Is he in command out there? Does his pitcher assume that whatever he throws is going to get hit?

The catcher takes into consideration the batter to his side. What are his strengths and weaknesses? What did he do last time up? Is he a first-ball swinger? Is he prone to taking inside fastballs? Does he look for outside pitches that he can punch into the outfield? Where are his feet? Is he hovering over the plate? Is he set back in the box? Does he have an open or closed stance? When the ball is released does he step toward the plate or away from it?

The catcher takes into consideration the umpire behind him. Does he have a high strike zone? A wide strike zone? Is he the type of umpire who will shrink a strike zone if the park has a working QuesTec machine? The catcher goes over all of these scenarios and more before he ever puts a finger down to call a pitch, and so despite having to squat close to twenty thousand times a year, it's not surprising that mental exhaustion often overshadows the physical pain. For all of the physical demands placed on a catcher, backstops who have played in the major leagues, almost to a man, say that the mental exertion is infinitely more fatiguing.

Jamie Quirk was a three-sport star in high school and received a football scholarship offer from Notre Dame. He played a variety of infield and outfield positions his first four major league seasons but converted to catcher at the suggestion of Whitey Herzog. Quirk played a total of eighteen seasons in the major leagues with more games behind the plate than any other position. He's currently the Colorado Rockies' bench coach.

"People ask me all the time," Quirk says, "what was the hardest part about it? The physical part? I say, No. The physical part was not hard. Blocking balls, taking balls off your legs. That comes with the territory. The hardest part was the mental part of getting the pitchers that you were catching believing that you knew what you were doing because you were new at it. You have to be there mentally every single day."

Like Quirk, catcher Ben Petrick has played a variety of positions in his five major league seasons. "It's a definitely a different position than any other on the baseball field," Petrick says. "It takes mental toughness. There's a lot going on when you're behind the plate, like knowing the hitter you're going up against, knowing the situation at that point in the game, how you're going to pitch that guy according to the scouting report and then putting it into that scenario of the game, whether it's the first inning, the ninth inning, the seventh inning, who's on second base. Knowing your pitcher, what stuff he has, what his mind makeup is like, and dealing with that part of the game. You're kind of a psychologist out there as much as anything. You put all that together and then you have to deal with having to actually catch the pitch or block the ball in the dirt. There's a lot of stuff going on."

Michael Barrett spent his career as a catcher for the Montreal Expos before joining the Chicago Cubs as their starting catcher in 2004, and for him, there's no question that, over the course of a season, the mental demands of the position are more fatiguing.

"It starts out as a physical battle," he says. "It starts out as a physical change. Your body goes through a metamorphosis. It just changes. You go through battles and physically the battle is over. You lost. There's nothing you can do about it, and that's when the mental side of the game is tough."

John Tamargo played five major league seasons with the Giants, Cardinals and Expos and served as the bench coach for the Houston Astros. Tamargo feels that catchers must be familiar with not only the demands of their position but those of every player on the entire field.

"Catchers are in all parts of the game," he says. "For instance, they've got to be able to handle the pitching, know different personalities, learn what pitchers do best in what situations. They have to know where the outfielders and infielders are playing. They have to know all the bunt plays. They're the only position that you can see everybody out on the field, when the ball's coming at you. On every pitch you're in the game. The game does not start until you put the signal down and the pitcher winds up.

"Catchers, from an early standpoint, learn to be part of the game. You learn to start thinking as a manager, or as a coach, as soon as you get back there. In certain situations you've got to know the next hitter, the next two hitters, whereas, let's say the outfielders are out there catching balls, and they're moving around and stuff, but you have to mentally be prepared for every inning, every situation, every hitter.

"You're thinking an inning ahead, most of the time. Who do they have up next inning? How are you going to handle those players? How are you going to pitch them? You don't want to get beat by this guy. He may be the fourth hitter in the inning. You don't want to get beat by this guy, so you might go after the hitter before a little more aggressively, then pitch around the next guy to get to the next guy. And, basically, that's what a catcher does. We have meetings all the time, pitcher and catcher meetings, telling them what we want to do with certain hitters, where we're going to play them, how we're supposed to pitch them and things like that. The catcher has to be involved in all of that. They have to know what their pitchers are capable of doing. And what they can't do."

"You know, I tried playing other positions," Mike O'Berry says. "I'd play the outfield just to do something, and I was bored to death."

Frank "Pig" House caught a total of ten big league seasons and roomed with Hall of Fame outfielder Al Kaline during his years in Detroit, and to this day is puzzled as to what the other fielders actually think about during a game.

"If you stop and think about it," House says, "it looks to me like the other ballplayers would get bored to death out there. I used to tell Kaline that he ought to have to pay to get into the ballpark. He may get one ball in right field for nine innings, while the catcher is involved in every pitch. It's exciting and I loved it."

Still, the mental part of the game takes its toll, especially at season's end.

"You're way more tired mentally," Todd Greene says. "If you catch a 1-0 game you're mentally beat after the game because there's a fine line for mistakes. If you catch an 11-10 game you're still beat up because you're trying to figure out, How in hell can I change this to get our pitchers back where they need to be to get these guys out? Either way you're beat up. It's absolutely tougher than the physical part. Even in the 110-degree heat of Texas."

Adam Melhuse, who has played four major league seasons and most recently with Oakland, has reached a stage where age and physical condition and their relevance to what's left of a career are more likely to preoccupy a catcher's mind.

ADAM MELHUSE

"Catching takes a lot out of you," Adam Melhuse says. "That's where you as a professional have to take care of yourself. I'm not going to lie. Early in the career, going out and stuff like that, that was all fine and dandy. You could have a long night and get up in the morning and bounce back like nothing happened when you're younger, but now that doesn't happen. You have to stay away from that. You have to get in the gym. You have to do your workouts. You have to do that stuff if you want to stay around. If you don't care, then do whatever you want. Healthwise, I haven't had any major problems, just little aches and pains here and there. Nothing a couple of Advil won't take care of.

"I don't feel thirty-one. I still feel young, and every now and again someone's like, 'Man, I thought you were twenty-seven, twenty-eight.' Stuff like that makes you feel good. I enjoy, in the off-season, lifting weights and getting in shape. I enjoy the challenge of pushing myself like that. Maybe I'm a little cuckoo. I guess you got to be a little cuckoo to be a catcher."

6TH

The Plays

Catchers, as a rule, have good memories. Most catchers have no trouble recalling pitch sequences from games twenty or thirty years before, and perhaps this shouldn't be surprising, because their job description requires knowledge of every hitter in the league.

But catchers remember more than pitch sequences. They also easily recall their first time in uniform, their first home run, which pitcher had the best fastball or the best curve. Catchers are also likely to remember the figurative train wrecks of their careers—the homeplate collisions.

No other player on the field partakes in more physical contact than the catcher (they're not wearing all that equipment to look good), and no other situation puts the catcher in harm's way like the collision at home plate.

In fact, the most difficult play for a catcher is the base hit to right field with a speedy runner on second base. When this happens, the catcher must receive the throw on his right side and tag the runner on his left, his blind side. It's not a rare occurrence for the ball and the runner to arrive almost simultaneously, or as Pete Rose would say, Bam! Bam!

On September 18, 1992, Atlanta Braves catcher Greg Olson was run over (literally) by Ken Caminiti of the Houston Astros. Olson suffered a fractured leg and a dislocated ankle when his lower body was caught underneath Caminiti in the collision at home plate. Olson managed to hang onto the ball, and Caminiti was called out to end the fourth inning of what would be a 13-3 loss, the Braves' worst defeat of the year, but Olson was sidelined for the rest of the season, including the Braves' World Series loss to the Blue Jays. With a roster spot open, the Braves called up minor leaguer Javy Lopez. It was Lopez's first time on a major league roster. In 1993, Greg Olson platooned with Damon Berryhill, but at the end of the year the Braves traded Berryhill and released Olson. Javy Lopez became the Braves starting catcher, a position he would hold for the next ten seasons. Greg Olson's major league career was over.

The Braves immediately increased their focus on catcher positioning for plays at the plate in the instructional league and spring training following Olson's injury. A young Joe Ayrault was in camp, three years before his major league debut.

"I think the biggest thing with the play at the plate," Ayrault says, "is staying low. Some guys keep their mask on, some guys keep their mask off. I always took mine off. I ended up getting some nice stitches in my chin, but that's personal preference. Just sacrifice your body. Do what you can do to save that run.

"Make sure your knee and your toe of your left foot are pointed straight down to third base. Make sure that everything on your left side is going straight toward third base, so if they slide into you at least you've got some give there.

"Basically I would start by having my heel right on that foul line, my toe pointed toward third. Obviously your upper body's going to be angled differently compared to where the ball's hit, center or right field, with right field being the toughest because you have to have that foot there. You stay open, but as the runner's coming in I always took an extra step deeper on the line, so it's actually not right on the foul line. Basically you're showing the runner home plate behind you, and you're hoping that if they slide they're going to go deep, and if they come into you you're going to take that step, one step deeper and stay low underneath them. That is definitely the key when you're getting smoked."

Ken Caminiti, the train that ran over Greg Olson, played bigger than the 6'0", 200 pounds he was listed. He won the National League MVP in 1996 while playing with the Padres. He hit 40 home runs, had 130 RBI and batted .326 for the year. After his retirement, Caminiti was one of the first former players to admit to using steroids during his career.

Ken Caminiti is also in the forefront of Bob Geren's mind. During Geren's playing career—four seasons with the Yankees and one with the Padres—he was listed as three inches taller and twenty pounds heavier than Caminiti, but Caminiti got the best of him during Geren's final season in 1993.

"I remember perfectly," Geren says. "The ball was in right field and the throw was a little up on the other side of the first base line where I caught it, a backhand on one bounce, and I felt like I had the time to dive back toward the plate. I had no idea he'd run into me. If he slid, actually, at the outside of the plate he'd have been safe. I'm five feet from the plate.

"I know it's going to be close, and I kind of turned and started almost a lunge toward the outside part of the plate, and he hit me in the right side and whiplashed my neck where it really affected my hitting. Actually it affected my whole year, I think. But it was clean. I was right in front of the plate. It was a pretty good hit. I mean, the whole right side of my body went numb. My neck was sore.

"You know, he came up his next at-bat, somewhat concerned as a professional, and he said, 'I just want to know if my hit was clean.' Maybe he wanted to know if we were going to drill him or something, who knows? But I said, 'No. It was clean.' It was a good hit. And he said, 'Nice job holding onto the ball.' Because he was actually out.

"I finished the game, and then the next day I could hardly move my neck, and I was in the lineup. I'd just got the starting job, and I was hitting about .260, and the next ten days, maybe, my average just went down, down,

down. I was having trouble getting my neck all the way on line to see the ball. But I'd just got the starting job. I wasn't going to tell anybody I didn't want to play, so I played through it. I just couldn't get that full range of motion. You're losing that extra ten or fifteen degrees of motion. If I was in any other job in the world it wouldn't have mattered, but to try to stay on line to see a baseball out of two eyes instead of one and three-quarter eyes was the key.

"Was I hurt?" Geren asks rhetorically. "No. I was just stiff. Football players are like that all the time. They get banged around a little bit. Hockey players probably feel that way all the time. So I really wasn't hurt. It didn't affect my catching. If I didn't have to hit, it would've been fine."

MIKE SCIOSCIA

Current Anaheim Angels manager Mike Scioscia was a two-time National League All-Star for the Los Angeles Dodgers. He never won a Gold Glove Award, but Scioscia is almost universally accepted as the best plate-blocker in major league history.

Though Scioscia's playing career lasted from 1980 to 1992, he was notoriously old school. He was a sturdy 6'2", 222 pounds, and facing off against him at home plate was not unlike going against the Green Bay

Packers defense in a goalline stand in mid-December.

Lance Parrish coached in the Los Angeles Dodgers system during the time Scioscia served as the organization's head catching instructor.

"His philosophy," Parrish says, "is one that you stand right in front of home plate, you catch the ball, and you drop to both knees and you just take the hit."

As a player, Parrish says, Scioscia "definitely laid himself out there. He certainly got his share of abuse, and because of that he's been labeled one of the best blockers of the plate, so I'll never take that away from him."

Though once knocked unconscious by the Cardinals' Jack Clark, Scioscia, for the most part, avoided serious injury from his home plate impacts. The same cannot be said for Lance Parrish.

"My knee got caught in a collision at home plate, and up until that point I felt that I was almost invincible," Parrish says. "That's what started all my problems.

"It was in '89 when I was catching with the Angels. We were playing Milwaukee in Milwaukee, and Glenn Braggs was the guy that ran into me. The ironic thing was there were two outs, and Joey Meyer, I believe, was the hitter. Glenn Braggs was on second base, and Joey Meyer hit a ball deep in the hole to short, between short and third. Dick Schofield went back and caught it and kind of double-clutched. He realized he probably wasn't going to have a chance to throw Joey out at first, even though Joey's a big man and didn't run that well. And Glenn Braggs, thinking that he was going to throw the

LANCE PARRISH

ball to first, never stopped at third. He just kept coming home.

"Well, Schofield realized that there was a play at the plate, so he threw the ball home and I had to reach up to catch the ball—I had to go high—and when I came down to try to get in position to make the tag it was like I just stepped toward the plate. I was almost down to where I was set and then he just plowed into me head first. It was almost like he was diving, and he hit my knee and it twisted it, and it burned.

"I'd never had any torn cartilage or anything like that so I really didn't know what it felt like, but I reasoned in my head, That must be what it feels like, because my knee felt like it was on fire. And I had a separated rib on my left side, so he got me pretty good. I tried to stay in the game and play, and it wasn't so much my knee at the time as much as my ribcage because I couldn't swing the bat. So I came out of the game and I had to take some time off, but I finished the rest of the season.

"I played with that for a few years until I couldn't stand it anymore because my knee was hurting all the time. It was suggested that I look into getting it scoped, and I've had it scoped twice, but the result of that is I'm bone on bone on the inside of my knee. And it hurts, just like anything would hurt. The more I do, the more I feel it. When I throw batting practice every day, that's my landing leg. And just that constant pounding and grinding on my landing leg for fifteen or twenty minutes every day, it starts to hurt a lot."

Because of his experience, Parrish has a different philosophy than Scioscia when it comes to teaching plate-blocking to young catchers.

"Live to see another day," Parrish says. "You're no use to your ballclub if you're injured. There is a proper technique to blocking the plate. If and when you can, on a perfect throw I guess, you put your foot on the line about a foot up from the plate. Point your toe toward third. Try to stay low. When you catch the ball, grab it with your bare hand.

"Mike would have guys catch the ball, drop to both knees and just slap-tag guys. Well, I've seen too many guys get the ball slapped out of their glove that way, so my teaching, the way I was taught, and I believe in this philosophy, is that when you catch the ball you try to get your bare hand on it and you apply the tag. If the guy does happen to hit you good enough to where it could possibly jar the ball loose, you've got the ball in your bare hand and it's not going anywhere. At least it shouldn't.

"But the object in trying to protect yourself in a collision is you want to try to get as low as possible. You don't want to make yourself vulnerable by standing upright or in a semi-upright position where you can get clocked. If you get down below the runner or stay down there with him, you're going to be able to absorb the hit, and most of the time he'll either roll you backward or you'll just stop him dead in his tracks.

"You also have to be smart," Parrish says, "in the sense that you have the ball and there's another way of making the tag without getting smoked at home plate. You apply the tag and just roll with them. Apply the tag and let him go. There's no sense in you hanging in there and getting run over every time. I've always taught that you try to give the runner part of the plate to shoot at. You give him something to see and normally they'll go for that. Most of the time they'll try to slide in headfirst or with their feet and try to catch that corner of the plate. But if you catch the ball early enough you can take that away from them. You can close the door on them and boom boom they're out. You want a guy to slide. You don't want a guy to run into you. So you try to give them every opportunity and something to shoot for in hopes that they'll get down on the ground."

Ten-year major league veteran Frank House doesn't need to have a good memory to recall the impact of a particularly violent home plate collision.

"I've got a very vivid picture. I mean, an actual photograph," he says. "Early in my career, the Philadelphia Athletics were still in Philadelphia, and they had a big outfielder by the name of Sam Chapman. Sam Chapman was about 6'5", 225, and a great All-American halfback from either Southern Cal or Cal. I never will forget it. They had a man on third, and Johnny Lipon was playing shortstop for us, and there was a ground ball hit to Johnny and he threw it where I had to reach up to get it. So I reached up, and about that time Chapman hit me. The picture shows very clearly that the ball is in the air to my left, the mitt is in the air over to the right, and my shin guards are spun around on my legs. It was quite a lick.

"Of course, it wasn't always their way. If a catcher can get the ball in time and they slide, they're dead. It's all over then. I remember Jackie Jensen, another great outfielder with the Boston Red Sox, and another All-American halfback from Cal or some place. One day, he came in and he slid. Well, all he got was shin guards, and those shin guards are hard. As he was laying there, he said, 'I've had all of those shin guards I want.'"

Like Frank House, Mike O'Berry has strong memories, as well as photographs, of home plate action.

"Probably the most violent collision," he says, "and thank God he wasn't a big guy, was when I was with the Angels. Wayne Tolleson, the little second baseman from Texas, was on first or second, there were two outs, and there was a little pop-up into right centerfield. The ball dropped amongst our center fielder and right fielder, and Ellis Valentine was playing right field. Probably one of the best arms in baseball. He picks it up, and Tolleson is running the whole way. He rounds third, and Ellis picks it up. He's not that far in the outfield, and Tolleson rounds third, so this play's going to be easy. Well, Ellis throws it almost straight down, and the ball rolls to the infield. I'm sitting in front of the plate, and I see

Tolleson out of my peripheral vision while I'm watching the ball. I'm talking about two feet before the ball gets to me, you know. I thought, I'm dead.

"I'm almost on both knees. I've got the plate blocked. He lowers his head and he runs right through the middle of my chest. I go completely in a back flip, and the ball rolls all the way to the backstop.

"He got me just before the ball got there. It was pretty neat. A guy took some pictures and he had the whole sequence of things. I've got some of them at home. Anyway, he hits me probably three feet in front of the plate and knocks me nearly out of the home plate circle. I kept my mask on. That's one thing I always did. Plays at the plate, I always kept my mask on. And so the ball rolled all the way to the backstop. Well, it knocked him out. He's laying out on the ground, two feet in front of the plate. The pitcher backing up the play throws it to Ron Jackson, the first baseman, and he tags Tolleson. They ended up having to carry him off on a stretcher with a neck brace, but that was probably as hard as I ever got hit."

Tennessee native Ed Bailey caught parts of fourteen seasons in the major leagues, primarily with the Cincinnati Reds. As a San Francisco Giant, he caught Hall of Fame pitcher Juan Marichal's only major league no-hitter. He was selected as an All-Star five times.

"Walt Moryn caught me not looking," Bailey says. "I'm still looking for him. If I could've ever gotten to him

I'd have run over him with a car. I was trying to make the play, and he got me from the side and I was looking for the ball. He got there a step ahead of the ball. The ball was coming from right field, and I was bent down trying to catch it. He nailed me. I was trying to block home plate from behind, trying to make him, if anything, slide on his wrong side to the inside part of the plate. It's the way I tried to make them slide. You slow them down a half-step or a step if you do that. And he didn't even break stride, much less slide. He got me all over."

After his fifteen seasons in the big leagues, Andy Seminick, nicknamed "The Mad Russian," coached up-and-coming catchers on home plate positioning.

"First of all," he says, "you try to get the runner to run into you, blocking the plate on a close play, head on. In other words, he's going to hit you in front. You're facing him. The play that's going to hurt you is the play coming from right field. You're going to have to have a chance to get your body turned around. You're going to be receiving the ball from the right side. You've got to get turned around in position where you're going to get hit head on, because if you don't, that's when you're going to get hurt.

"Of course, we teach young catchers to plant their foot with their toe pointed right at third base, so when you get hit you get hit that way instead of having your toe at second base or something like that. That's how I got hit. I didn't get my foot turned around in time.

"When I first came up I had a hard time tagging players out. They'd always be sliding around me. They told me to give the runner part of the plate, but I would always miss them and they would slide around me. So I decided to get right over the plate, to have the plate right between my feet, because that way I'll be right there and they couldn't be sliding around me. That's how I finally figured it out."

Seminick's studied approach, however, did not mean he wasn't involved in more than his share of home plate confrontations.

"Pee Wee Reese ran into me one time when I wasn't turned around right," he says. "I was up the line. He came in standing up and hit me in the side of the jaw, and kind of turned me a flip. I was spitting out teeth for a while. His hip hit me right in the jaw. I thought I blocked the plate good, but you've got to get yourself turned around where he's running into you instead of on the side of you, and sometimes that doesn't happen."

But the meeting with Reese is not Seminick's most noted home plate impact. Like Greg Olson and Bengie Molina, who suffered a broken wrist at the end of his 2003 Gold Glove season, Seminick was hit hard in a late-season game. After numerous run-ins with Eddie Stanky of the Giants, on September 27, 1950, Seminick was involved in a home plate conflict with another New York player.

"It was in the last week of the season," he says. "Monte Irvin was the winning run in the tenth inning, and I blocked the plate and he ran into me and broke my leg. He was on second base. Alvin Dark was the hitter, and of course Alvin Dark was a great ballplayer and a good hitter. He was a right-handed hitter, and he hit the ball to right field. That's usually the play that really gets the catcher in trouble. You try to get your body in a position where you're not going to be on the side or anything. You try to get where he's going to hit you straight on. This time the ball was hit to right field, and I didn't get turned around soon enough. And Monte Irvin just crashed into me. He hit me pretty good on my left leg and it twisted.

"It was a good throw, and I thought I had him out, but the umpire said different. I saw pictures of it later, and I did block him off the plate. He slid off to the left of the plate, but I thought I had him tagged out."

X-rays later revealed a bone separation in his ankle, but Seminick played in all four games of what would be his only post-season appearance as the Yankees swept his Phillies four games to none in the 1950 World Series.

7TH

The Stories

During the interviews conducted for this book, common themes arose—various stories about similar subjects and situations ranging from how they began their careers to how they ended them. In this chapter, you'll hear the stories directly from the catchers.

The Road to the Show

I loved baseball. I was a die-hard as a kid. I grew up with my just my mom and sister. My dad was in New York. Detroit was my favorite team growing up. I was born in Rochester, Michigan, and those were the first major league games that I went to, at the old Tiger Stadium. My dad and my relatives were around the Detroit area so whenever I'd visit they'd always take me to baseball games there at Tiger Stadium, so that's what I remember.

Lance Parrish was always my favorite catcher. I always looked up to him. He was like my mentor. You think how enormous he was, especially to a kid. You look at him, he's just a monster, and he was the Tigers catcher. I had the Tiger catcher poster in my room, the Lance Parrish glove growing up, had all his baseball cards. I met him at a celebrity softball game. I won something where I could be the bat boy. All these major leaguers came to Sarasota, and Parrish sat next to me, and he signed every single baseball card that I had of him. He was such a great guy.

Actually there's a funny story. I was in major league camp in 1995, I believe, and I had a baseball card of Lance Parrish in my car, and Terry Clark, a pitcher—he's now in Nashville as the pitching coach—he says, What are you doing with that thing? And I said, "Hey, that's my favorite player growing up. It kind of reminds me of my childhood, so when I'm going to the park or something it just brings back memories."

He says, "I know Lance pretty well. He's a good friend of mine. I work out with him. I said, "No way." So later that night I'm sitting in my hotel room, and the phone rings. Clarky answers the phone and hands it to me. He says, "It's for you." I said, "Hello?" A voice says, "Joe, this is Lance Parrish." I was like, Get out of here, you know. He said, "No, really it is." I turned and looked at Clarky. I wanted to shoot him I was so embarrassed. And I sat there and talked to him for about fifteen minutes. Told him where I was at and stuff. Talked to him for a while. It was great.

–Joe Ayrault

I started out playing shortstop and second base in Little League. I had a good arm, so I stayed in the infield. But my coach and my dad in my senior year of high school told me I should switch to catcher, thinking I could go further that way. I had tried to improve my running speed in high school, with track coaches and stuff, and I did improve a little bit but not enough to get to the next level, not as a middle infielder. Maybe as a third baseman but then who knows? At third base you really have to hit in the minor leagues.

– *Mike Lieberthal*

I would've signed for a dollar. I wanted to play baseball. I just wanted to follow in my brother's footsteps, you know. Since he went to play minor league ball, I wanted to do the same thing. I would've signed for free.

– *Mandy Romero*

My first few games were as a shortstop, and then our catcher got hurt and no one else wanted to catch. So I went behind the plate without a protective cup or anything on, which is not the brightest thing to do, but I wanted to play. The moment I got behind there I loved it because I had all the responsibility. I was in charge of calling the game. I was in charge of moving guys around. If I thought guys were out of position and I wanted to make a certain pitch or a certain hitter was up and the guy, I felt, was out of position, I could always move him around.

– *Elrod Hendricks*

Andy Seminick, who was a tough Russian, taught me, more or less, how to block home plate. Walker Cooper was my idol. I went up to Cincinnati, and I wound up rooming with my idol in the first spring training that I ever went to with the Reds. And he taught me so much it was unreal. I couldn't even tell you what all. And then I had Bob Scheffing as a coach, you know, and then I had Birdie Tebbetts as a manager.

I had catching coaches, if you want to say that. Their fundamentals, some of them vary a little bit, and you've got to figure out what works the best for you. It's as simple as that. But I tell you, Tebbetts was tough. In fact, if you did something he'd say, "Why?" And you'd have to answer him. You know, "Why?" He wasn't always asking to be smart. He wanted to know for himself why you did it that way. Whether it was good or bad. Why?

– Ed Bailey

The Tigers drafted me first. I think Detroit offered me something like a ten-thousand-dollar signing bonus. And I said, "No, I'll stay in school." They really weren't pushing it. I guess the guy just drafted me because they needed to use up a draft pick or something. I don't know. The following year the Yankees drafted me, and they didn't even offer me any money.

At the junior college level, we were there to play. I did it because I enjoyed it. I was there to get an education, and I got an education there for two years. Stuck straight to the books. I probably had a high A average. I wasn't worried. I never even thought about it. And then when I went to Alabama there were more people in the stands. There were scouts. I started thinking maybe I can play at the next level. I think Dick Howser was with ESPN at the time. They'd just started doing college baseball, and he did a little segment with me about wooden bats compared to aluminum bats, because we used the wooden bats up until that year. And afterwards he talked to me about the next level. It kind of started sticking to me then. When the Cardinals drafted me that year, I never even knew they were there.

Marty Myers, who was the scout at the time, said something like, "We want to offer you a bona fide contract." Well, he never did even talk about money when we first picked him up at the airport, and we got home and he came to talk to Mama and Daddy, and he said, "We're going to give him ten thousand dollars," and my heart left me again.

And the next morning about six o'clock he called and said, "I got a hold of the front office. Tell me what you're wanting." And I said, "I'd like to at least have it worth my while to leave here." He said, "You've got to give me a number." It was like car dealing. He said, "We'll meet you halfway," and I said, "Fine, let's go." From that point on, you realize that you're not playing for fun no more. It's an income. It all got serious from that point on.

– Randy Hunt

May 11 is the day I signed the contract in '65. I wasn't drafted. Didn't sign for a lot of money. Plane ticket, a catcher's mitt, a pair of spikes, five hundred dollars. It was more money than I ever had, you know. I'll put it like this. My aunt, she needed the help, and I knew that if I went to college she couldn't afford sending me money or whatever. So I put it this way. If the man came after baseball, I'm going to go play baseball. But if he don't, then I'll go off to Alabama State. I looked at my aunt, and she didn't know anything about negotiations and I didn't either. I looked at my uncle. He didn't know anything about no contract. And so they just said, "Sign."

I look at it this way. It's money. Everything revolves around it. That's what makes the world go round. They didn't have any money invested in me. I'm going to give you a good example. We're going to go back to that five hundred dollars. I thought I had some money. And we got to Bradenton, Florida, during the little spring training session. Do you remember the envelopes with the red, white, and blue? The business envelope with the red, white, and blue all the way around the rim? Everybody got a letter that day, and the letter was from Houston. So I got my letter, looked at it. Five hundred dollars. Boy, I'm happy. I looked over my right shoulder. He got fourteen thousand dollars. I looked over here and he got twenty thousand dollars. I said, "How in the hell did they get this kind of money?" They weren't no better than I was.

– *Otis Thornton*

My wife got word to me that the Indians were going to invite me to spring training. So I went to Tucson coming out of Mexico. In those days there were no jets. So you flew all the way to Cincinnati and about three weeks later you had to fly back to Tucson. Al Lopez was the manager of the ballclub, and we had a back room down there. They had a boiler room. Guys like us, the first year invitees, weren't allowed in the clubhouse, so we were in the boiler room. Well, in that boiler room there was Gary Bell, Jim Perry, Mudcat Grant, myself, Gordy Coleman and about five others. Within two years we're all in the big leagues, but Lopez kept us down there. Gave us only one at-bat. I'll never forget—I got one at-bat against Steve Ridzik. I walked and he picked me off first just like that. That was the only at-bat I got. So Lopez took us there, gave us one at-bat and shipped us all out. We flew all the way back to Daytona Beach from Tucson.

So now we get down there and they start forming the ballclubs and I make the Triple A club. I hit .320, I think, in Triple A, a nice year, and next thing I know I'm on a boat going to Havana. Family and everything. The kids. All of us going on the boat, and that was the great time in my life, playing in Havana, Cuba, in the winter of '56-'57.

There's where they separate the men from the boys. We had Camilo Pascual. Several Cuban pitchers, major league pitchers. And Jim Bunning was pitching down there. Paul Foytack. A lot of guys that went to the big leagues and then established themselves were in the league. There were only four clubs and we played four games a week, but that's where you really got a feel for what you had to do to become a major league player.

I didn't hit all that well. I hit probably .260 down there, but they invited me back the next year, and I think I led the league in hitting. Anyway, those two years in Cuba were probably the foundation of getting to the big leagues because there wasn't anything left unturned.

– *Russ Nixon*

We were playing in Rochester one time, and Stan Musial had just joined their club. Back in those days the catcher watched the other team take batting practice to see if he could pick up anything, particularly when they had a new guy. And I snuck out of the clubhouse while they were hitting, and boy he looked like a hitter to me. I said, "I don't know how the hell to pitch this guy." His first couple of times at bat he hung out frozen ropes, I remember that very well.

– *Buddy Hancken*

You know what the Braves did? In my second year they sent me to Burlington, Iowa, and I was the only Spanish guy on the team. Now I say I'm glad they did it, because that's the only way I learned a lot of English, but back then I was furious. I wanted to go home.

The beginning was tough, because I had the idea but I didn't know how to say it. I can tell you when they sent me to that team I was mad. I was pissed. I was like, I'm going home. But now, I'm glad they did so. The American guys helped me a lot. I lived with them. I spent the whole day with them, and you either learn the language or go on home, and I did learn a lot.

–Eddie Perez

Things were going well. I was getting a chance to play a little third base. That went really well. Behind the plate went well. And offensively I swung the bat well, so I figured they only had one left-handed bat on the bench, and I knew that they were looking for another one, and out of the possible candidates I thought I had a great shot because I was a catcher and I showed them that I could play some third base and first base as well. So it went up to that very last day in San Francisco, and they informed me that it was just a roster move, that they had decided to go with Ron Gant, with some veteran leadership on the bench, and Adam Piatt was out of options, and they weren't ready to lose him yet, so it was just one of those things where I got squeezed out.

It took me a good two or three days to really shake out of it and look at what I had ahead of me and that type of thing. I spent the whole off-season preparing—lifting weights, hitting, everything else—and in spring training I did everything I could, and when it doesn't work out it's just a huge letdown. It would've been one thing if I knew, or if I felt like I wasn't having a good spring. Then it would've been a different story, but to go up to the last day. My gut feeling was telling me that I was going to be on that team, and then to hear otherwise was just, I mean, it was just like shock.

– *Adam Melhuse*

Making the Majors

I knew I was going to have a pretty good chance, to be honest with you. This is going to sound crazy, but when I walked into the clubhouse and saw my number, I saw McCarver had number six, and I had number seven. That's a pretty good indication, I found out. When I first started going to big league camps you got, like, number sixty-five, you're on the end of the row, way back around the corner. Then you come in and all of a sudden you're on the regular row with everybody else. You say, "Oh, wait a minute. Look at my number." And you think, Wow, I may actually have a chance of making the team this year.

– *Mike Compton*

The manager of Houston at the time, [Leo] Durocher, told me I was going to be there for the rest of the season. And Bull Watson said, "Otis, you're here for the rest of the season." So we went back to Houston. Had my first wife and my son—he was a toddler then—and me and Jim Wynn went to the airport that morning and picked them up. That afternoon I got dressed, walked through the tunnel, got to the very top step and was fixing to put my foot on the top step and then my other foot was going to step on the AstroTurf. Somebody said, "Otis, Leo wants to see you." And I turned around and went back and Leo said, "We're sending you back to Denver." I said, "You told me in New York that I was going to be here the rest of the season." He said, "Well, Johnny Edwards is back so if you stay here you won't be playing. We don't want you just sitting up here.

– *Otis Thornton*

I had a pretty good spring. I threw it real well, and hit decent. I think the game that made it was when we played the Dodgers over at Dodgertown. I threw [Davy] Lopes out a couple of times and got a couple of hits.

It was kind of funny. I think [Walt] Hriniak was the first one that said something to me. It was up to the last couple of days before anything was ever really decided, and finally there were twenty-five of us left.

[Don] Zimmer didn't say a whole lot. It was the last couple of days, and they cut and they cut, and there were twenty-five of us left, and they started calling around saying things like, "This is what we're going to do." And they started talking about flying, trying to get people to drive your car to Boston for you and stuff like that. That's the way we made the team. It was kind of like you were just in the group.

– *Mike O'Berry*

I was out on the golf course when they come and got me. Baseball players, in general, are notorious for playing practical jokes. And the trainer told me I was in trouble with the coach, Jim Fregosi. I was with the Louisville

Redbirds, Triple A. Playing in Iowa against the Cubs.

About 11:30, twelve o'clock he comes up to the seventeenth hole, right before I'm finishing and just says, "Get in." I'm not knowing anything. He won't tell me anything. I walk in the motel, and there's Jim Fregosi sitting there. And he says, "I told you if you mess up one more time you're out of here. Get your stuff and get ready."

I was a problem child, but I wasn't that bad a problem. I wasn't in jail and stuff like that, but I was always on Fregosi's list. You had to walk a straight line with Jim Fregosi. He was a manager that when you walked out on the field he expected 100 percent, and if you weren't 100 percent then he let you know. That's just the way he was. And I was notorious for playing practical jokes. I could play them just as good as the next guy. Nobody was spared. I'd play a practical joke on Jim Fregosi. Nobody was off-limits to me. In that respect, I had several of those run-ins.

I never questioned him ever, so I turned and walked towards the elevator and he says, "Oh, by the way. You're going to St. Louis." And I'm like, "Oh, you sorry thing." Darrell Porter was the catcher in St. Louis at the time. He'd gotten a foul tip, broke his finger. So I loaded up and headed to the airport. I think I had twenty dollars to my name. Last day of the road trip and all. Pulled into St. Louis and got in a taxi, and it was something like eighteen dollars already on the cab fare, and I told the guy, I said, "Buddy, how much further we got to go? I've got twenty dollars to my name." He said, "Listen. You're going to the big leagues. Don't worry about this one."

It was just one of those things. Once I got out of the cab and walked in the clubhouse, they accept you. It doesn't matter who they are. I mean, at that time you had Bob Forsch, Darrell Porter, Ozzie Smith, all those guys. You're walking in, and you've already spent spring training with them, so it's not really a total scare, but everybody's just glad to see you, and saying, "Hey, you got to hurry up. It's already seven o'clock. It's a 7:30 game."

I didn't play that night, but the next night Tom Nieto, first pitch of the game, took a foul tip off his knee, and I remember running across there. I felt like it may've taken me four or five steps to run from the bullpen to the dugout because that's how emotional I was. Just adrenaline flowing. My parents and all, I knew they were there. It's just the most unbelievable thing you could ever experience. You see it, but until you live it you can't explain it. It's just an adrenaline rush that is unbelievable.

– *Randy Hunt*

I was in the Southern League, Knoxville, and it was my birthday. It was the time of [World War II], and I had been called up to go to the Army in the next call, which was in September. Then Bill Veeck called and told me he had sold me to Philadelphia. He wanted me to report. I said, "I can't. I'm going in the service." It was like the next week or something. He said, "You got to go. You got to report." We kept talking and finally he says, "If you report I'll have a check there for you, a five-hundred-dollar check. So, of course, being young and married at the time, I went to the man in charge of the service call-up, and I explained the situation to him, and he said, Well, you go ahead and we'll get you in the next call-up. So I called Veeck back and told him I was going. That's how I found out I was in the big leagues. That was on my birthday.

– *Andy Seminick*

Debuts

I kind of got yelled at by Billy Martin my first game I ever caught. It was brutal.

I remember sitting in Billy's office and them going over the advance scouting report on Oakland—it's McGwire, Canseco, Don Baylor. They talked about a lot of sliders and breaking balls. I just remember perfectly what they said about Baylor. You could get in on him occasionally, you know. So you could throw a slider, and then you could open up and throw a fastball inside. He likes to get his arms extended. Big, strong guy. Billy just chimed in, Don't get it too far in. The guy will just let it hit him. Because, you remember, Baylor had all the hit-by-pitches.

I came in the game and Tim Stoddard, who was a ten-year veteran, was pitching. I was a ten-minute veteran, and the hitter before was either Canseco or McGwire. I think Canseco was batting fourth, Baylor fifth. And Stoddard threw Canseco probably three out of four sliders, and all three were not even close to the strike zone and he walked him. So when Baylor came up

I remembered Martin saying—I mean, verbatim; I could quote the guy, what he said—a lot of sliders. He chases this and that. So I started thinking, I'm going to put a slider down. Then I thought, Part of the report said he was a good first-ball hitter. So I started thinking about putting a slider down, then I realized if he throws a slider it's going to be ball one. You're really even a better hitter 1 and 0 than you are on a first pitch. If you throw a breaking ball out of the zone by two feet on the first pitch your percentage of getting a fastball on the next pitch goes way up. So I just figured, I'm going to go right to the fastball inside.

There was a runner on first and second and two out, and we're losing 7-4, something like that. It wasn't a real close game. And he broke his bat, looped it right over the shortstop in that big area in left center. Just dunked it in for a single, and Billy came to the mound, and I went out there. I thought he was going to take Stoddard out or say something to him, but he started yelling at me on the mound. "What are you doing? Don't you listen to my reports?" He was so angry.

You know, I played ten years in the minor leagues before I got up, so when I came back to the dugout I'm thinking, Ten years to get here, and now after ten minutes I'm going to be going back tomorrow. I was pretty upset, and then Joel Skinner, the other catcher, and Don Slaught, the other catcher who was on the DL, they both came up to me and started laughing. I don't remember what I said. Something like, "That's not funny." I was kind of mad. And they said, "Hey, he does that to everybody." They surrounded me. They said, "Don't worry about it. Welcome to New York. Welcome to the big leagues."

But I didn't play again. I had maybe an inning here or there, a couple of pinch-hits or whatever. After that Billy ended up not being the manager, and the next year I played quite a bit. He was the TV analyst and shortly before his death I saw him at a card show, and he had said something like, "I watched you play last year. I really liked the way you call the game. You did a good job." That made me feel real good, because that's what I felt like I did best. That was something where you don't have to have a great arm, you don't have to have great speed, you don't have to have a lot of ability. You just have to soak up the game. There's a knowledge you learn. You put time into studying hitters and pitchers and learning, and so when he said that I felt a lot better.

– *Bob Geren*

It was kind of, you know, a dream that just came true. I got my debut, first base hit, first at-bat. I think there was one out. I was on first base, and if you ask me about the last two outs, I don't really remember. I wasn't even on the field. I was just dreaming how I got there and all the stuff that I went through, so it was about the greatest feeling in the world.

– *Humberto Cota*

We're in Philadelphia, old Shibe Park, and I had become one of the best negotiators for autographed baseballs in the bullpen. I could get three, four hot dogs and a couple peanuts and stuff like that for guys. So we're doing that because in Philadelphia we're way off to the side. Then the phone rings. It was in the top of the ninth when [Joe] Torre got a base-hit, they pinch-ran for him, phone rang and the guy said, "Bart, you're in there next inning." I couldn't believe it. I ran down, put the gear on, and when the inning was over we got out to the plate, and I'm warming up the guy, and the umpire leans over and he says, "Nervous?" I said, "Nervous? My frigging knees are shaking." He said, "Kid, happens to everybody. Relax. Enjoy this. It's a moment you'll always remember." And it just helped me to relax. So the inning was over before we knew it because they got a base-hit, a sacrifice, strike out, base-hit, and the game's over.

I was on the on-deck circle twice to pinch-hit early in the season, and there was two outs once, and one out once, and I thought maybe this was going to be it, but the guy was on second base, a line drive to center, guy makes the catch, guy on second took off and they double him off. So that's twice that I had maybe an opportunity, but it wasn't made to happen.

I was just happier than hell to have made the team, to have been a part of it. Did I want to get in? Did I want to get my at-bat? Absolutely. On the other hand, the reality is you got to know where you are, and my place was—they made it fairly clear to me—that Joe [Torre] was going to be the workhorse for fifty days until [Ted] Simmons came back, and then he was going to go to third base and Simmons was going to take over. So that's the way it works.

I remember once when I was in Chicago, when we came up to Chicago, and they had me on one of the leadoff shows, just a quick interview, and they said, "So how does it feel to be the twenty-fifth guy on the Cardinals? Without thinking I said, "I'll tell you what, it feels a lot better than being the first guy in Tulsa." I remember Louie Boudreau saying, "Absolutely." And don't ever think differently.

– *Bart Zeller*

The deal was, as they told us, at least me in spring training, that Mike Ryan was going to be traded, and that Timmy McCarver and I were going to catch. Before spring training was over, Mike broke his thumb. He broke it or it was badly messed up. So that just took him out of the picture, so naturally then I've got to go north. There's no competition at that time, because Mike's injured.

So I start with the club, and I'm there until whenever Mike recovers, and then somehow they had to bring Mike back on the roster, to clear waivers or something, so I was gone like five days. They sent me to Eugene. I was there five days, and then he and McCarver both were in a game in San Francisco, and they both get their hands broken so I go back up. I had to fly to San Francisco and play immediately. I just got there and basically walked out on the field to play. I was catching every day.

– *Mike Compton*

The first game I caught in the big leagues I caught Bob Lemon in Kansas City, and Lemon's stuff was about shot. We got our asses kicked. His arm was bothering him. In those days you pitched through all that stuff. There wasn't any operation to speak of to correct it, and at his age he wasn't about to do that anyway. But he got pelted that day, and it was my first game catching. The first thing the press asked him was, "Did the kid catching back there affect you?" And he said, "Hell no. He wasn't throwing the goddamn ball."

– *Russ Nixon*

Calling the Game

Before I ever called a pitch, the first thing I did was look at the hitter's feet. I found that the hitter unconsciously would tell you a lot about what he was thinking was coming. If he thought that you were going to pitch him inside, and maybe hard stuff inside, he would click the dirt off his shoes and get pine tar. They readjust the hitting gloves and all that. They're out there doing a little thinking. And when they come in and set up, they'll set up a little deeper in the box, and maybe a little farther off the plate, or open up just a little bit. It might only be an inch or so, but if you look you'll see there's a difference. If they think you're going to an off-speed pitch, they may move up a little bit. Or if you're going to go outside, they'll be toed in a little bit. They'll close the stance just a little bit. It's funny. They might start out balanced, but as they start taking some practice swings they'll start working their way to that position. It's weird, but they almost let you read their minds.

– *Mike Compton*

If things are going well the pitcher's going to get all the credit, which he should, because obviously he's doing a nice job. I think catchers earn their money calling games when the pitcher doesn't have good stuff. You find a way—and he might only go four or five innings—but you find a way to keep him in that game, keep your team in the game when he doesn't have anything out there. The fans say, "This guy had a tough start. He gave up four runs in four innings." But you know what? That catcher probably did a good job of limiting the damage. You got him to the bullpen, you kept your team in the game. Those are the games that a catcher really shows up. When a guy has dominant stuff, it's easy back there.

– *John Flaherty*

I looked at it by the way the batter stands in the batter's box. That's where I set up. When they're taking their practice swings, I'm looking how far that bat is covering the plate. If the barrel of the bat is covering the whole plate, we've got a problem. So I'm going to go inside to see if he's going to handle this ball inside. I tell the pitcher, "Wherever I go, you hit me. If I go in there, if he can't handle it, then he's got a problem. He's going to back off of that plate to get a better look at the ball, and once he backs off, now I go outside with the same pitch."

You have to set him up. If he's set deep back in the box, he's looking for strictly fastballs. That's going to give him a better view of the ball, so now you give him something that looks like a fastball, but it's not. That's the slider. It's going to come there and then it's going to move to the outside. Now, I'm still watching his feet. If he takes a half a step up, then I'm going to bust his ass inside with a fastball. He's going to try to catch the slider before it breaks, either the slider or the curveball before it breaks. But you just don't throw him a slider, a curveball, a slider. You've got to think. On each pitch that you throw you've got to think about where you're going to put the ball. The pitcher is going to have to stay ahead of the batter. Your first pitch is going to have to be a strike. You're not just out here throwing the ball. Make every pitch count. If you go back and talk to some of your pitchers, when they got smarter is when they lost their arm. They got smarter.

– *Otis Thornton*

The best teachers, believe it or not, are veteran pitchers that know how to pitch. Or, if you're smart enough, you learn from your mistakes. I remember not having a catching instructor, but I remember playing against veteran players—guys like Ozzie Virgil, Sr. and Vic Power. They'd set me up as a young kid catching early in the ballgame. I'd call for a breaking ball without realizing that these guys could no longer catch up to good fastballs so they became breaking ball hitters. They'd look terrible. So I thought, When I need an out, I'll go to that. Well, when that time came they were ready for me to call that pitch and as soon as I called it they rifled the ball into right center and got to second base and looked at me. You know, like, "I got you, kid." After two or three of those I said, "I've been duped for the last time. This is not going to happen again." I learned that way, and I was fortunate enough to play winter ball and learn from guys like Ruben Gomez, who was one of the smartest pitchers I caught before I got to the big leagues.

Even when I got to the big leagues at age twenty-seven, I sat on the bench and listened to what George Bamberger had to say. And I learned from him. He made little statements like, "If a guy throws a breaking ball 3-1 for a strike, if you can throw it 3-1 you can do it 3-2." But he was saying it to nobody in particular. He was just saying it out there so everybody could hear. He wanted his pitchers to know that it's okay, if you have the confidence to throw a pitch over 3-1 you can do it 3-2. And that made them a lot better. They started having confidence without even doing it out there. They felt that if I called a 3-1 breaking ball and they threw it over, I could go back to it right away without even thinking about it, and they had enough confidence to throw it over. That's what made that [Orioles] staff a good staff.

– *Elrod Hendricks*

It's what you did with your hands. You took the inside of the thigh, or sometimes you flip them, like the thumb. You just do a thumb, like you're flipping a coin. That means, "Hey, flip this guy." We probably used that as much as anything. We just flipped the thumb back in those days, and that meant, "Hey, we're going to turn this guy upside down."

– Mike Compton

To be a good catcher, you've got to make adjustments. A good catcher watches what the hitters do every time up. They're aware of what they threw him the last at-bat, how they started them off, maybe even the pattern they've fallen into with every guy. I'm conscious of a guy when he comes up the third time, what I started him with the first two times, how it worked. You're watching. You're reading his swings, how he's taking pitches. If he's fouling the ball, which way is he fouling it? Then you're watching the guy's feet. Maybe he's moving in the box. Maybe you've been beating inside all day, and he's moved off the plate and now he's looking for something inside. It's something you can't see in the stands or the dugout, but I can see that behind the plate. Sometimes even the pitcher doesn't see it. So maybe I'll put down a sign two times or just pat my chest to tell him I know something and to throw this pitch. I think it really helps. My main goal is to get that pitcher through that game and make him be the best he can be and get us a win. It's all about wins.

– Tim Laker

The First Home Run

We had a coach named Ted Lyons. Great guy. Big, hard-throwing right-handed pitcher for the White Sox years before. He was our first base coach, and he had an alarm watch. I'd never seen an alarm watch. He always used it. Like if a bus was supposed to leave, he'd set that watch, and when the watch went off you'd better be on the bus because that's when the bus was leaving.

And I wasn't playing much. I said, "Give me that watch. I want that watch." He never had been married, and he was always the one who would buy the rookie pitchers a glove and a pair of shoes. Anyway we spent a long time talking about that watch and finally he told me, "If you hit a home run before the year's over, I'll give you this watch." And so later in the year [Steve] Gromek was pitching, and he throws me a fastball, and I hit it in the upper deck. Barely into the upper deck, but when I tell the story in front of Gromek it hit off the facing of the third deck. Of course I was numb by the time I got to first base, but Lyons was laughing, and I remember he said, "I'll give it to you when we get in the clubhouse." I went around the bases excited and thrilled, and got the watch. It won the ballgame for us 7-6.

I've had that watch fifty-two years. I don't know how long he'd had the watch, but I've got it. It usually sits right by my bed. It's something, my daughter, I'll know she'll keep it.

– *Frank House*

It was in Chicago, when I was playing with Montreal. I hit it 415 feet. I remember everything. Ron Davis hung a slider in my face, and I hit the daylights out of it, and threw the bat up in the air like you're not supposed to do, and Tim Raines was ragging me as soon as I got back to the dugout. Here's a guy who had never hit a home run, and he's watching it go out. Everybody hits one in Chicago, Harry Caray said after I'd hit that home run. I've got it taped. How come the first home run anybody ever hits is always against the Cubs in Chicago? And it's pretty much that way, it seems like. But I got my name in the books. I got one.

When you jog around the bases in a major league ballpark with fifty thousand people standing there, and you know it's on TV—you know your parents are watching, you know everybody in Montgomery, back home, is watching—it's just an adrenaline rush. As soon as you hit first base you think, They're seeing this. Don't fall flat on your face. You're thinking, Left foot, right foot. It's one of those deals. It's great.

– Randy Hunt

Catching a No-Hitter

Allie Reynolds, 1-0 vs. Cleveland Indians on July 12, 1951

Allie Reynolds, 8-0 vs. Boston Red Sox on Sept. 28, 1951

Don Larsen, 2-0 vs. Brooklyn Dodgers on Oct. 8, 1956

Everybody's aware that a no-hitter's going on. They know it. But you never say anything to a guy. Like, you know, when Reynolds and Larsen threw them, you don't talk to them. You might jinx them. I caught three of them, the two Reynolds and the Larsen.

– *Yogi Berra*

Virgil Trucks, 1-0 vs. Washington Senators on May 15, 1952

Everybody knew that he had a no-hitter. Everybody got a little tense, including, I'm sure, Virgil, and including myself. And we just went along and went with the fastball and the hard slider, and he was getting everybody out, and sure enough there wasn't really a ball hit very hard.

We wouldn't fool around with the change or a curveball or anything like that. Just a fastball and a slider and that was it. A hard slider and a hard fastball, and Virgil just let it go as hard as he could, and he was throwing strikes. That was the main thing.

– *Joe Ginsberg*

Jim Bunning, 3-0 vs. Boston Red Sox on July 20, 1958

First of all, it was in Boston, which is more of a hitter's park than most parks—short left field fence, not too long down the right field line. Bunning was not at all superstitious about talking about a no-hitter, so when he got into about the fifth and sixth inning of the no-hitter he was talking. He was bringing the subject up. It's a superstition that everyone kind of knows, and surely if Bunning had not thrown the no-hitter, it might've been thrown up in his face.

We figured out that if anyone got on base, or there was a hit, that [Ted] Williams would come up to bat in the ninth. He would be the tenth batter from the time we had it figured out when he batted last. I think it was either late in the eighth inning or in the ninth inning, Bunning hit Jackie Jensen with a pitch, which set up the fact that Williams was going to come up to bat in the ninth, which he did. Of course it was like Casey coming to bat. There was a lot of electricity in the air. Everybody knew there was a no-hit game on the line.

As I recall, the count went to two and two, and I'm trying to figure what he should throw. He was primarily a fastball and slider pitcher. His curveball was not his best pitch, although to right-handers he had a big sweeping curveball that could be effective. But Williams was, at least in his prime, more of a fastball hitter. At any rate, I'm trying to figure out what to call. Of course, Bunning pitched this whole game too, but as a catcher you try to help, whatever you can do. Bunning threw him the hard slider, which Williams hit pretty good. It looked like it might even go out of the park towards right field, but it didn't have enough on it, and Kaline caught the ball for the last out in the ninth.

– *Red Wilson*

Juan Marichal, 1-0 vs. Houston Colt .45s on June 15, 1963

He comes to the ballpark with a 103 fever and he told Larry Jansen, our pitching coach, that he was sick, that he didn't want to pitch. Alvin Dark tried to talk to him, but Juan said, "Skip, I'm just sick as a dog." At any rate,

Larry Jansen says, "You'd better go talk to your boy over there. He said he's sick. He doesn't want to pitch."

I sat down with him and said, "Juan, do me a favor. Go out there and go as hard as you can as far as you can. You're the only pitcher we've got that could be ready. Go out there and go as hard as you can as far as you can. We've got Don Larsen or Stu Miller who can pick you up." He didn't need any help. Pitched a no-hitter. And there wasn't a ball hit hard off of him.

– *Ed Bailey*

Steve Busby, 3-0 vs. Detroit on April 27, 1973

Steve Busby, 2-0 vs. Milwaukee on June 19, 1974

Catchers have nothing to do with it. If catchers had something to do with it, they'd catch two hundred of them. Busby's no-hitter in Detroit: you know, he was a kid, relatively speaking. His first year in the big leagues. He's the only guy that did it his first and second year in the big leagues, only guy in the history of the game to do that. He had good stuff, he had very good stuff, but he was throwing it, I was catching it, and we were hoping. The second one he was throwing and knew he could do it, and when I was catching him I knew he could do it. But I had nothing to do with it. No catcher does. I mean, Jeff Torborg caught five of them or something. [Sandy] Koufax, [Nolan] Ryan and [Bill] Singer. Nobody could hit Koufax, nobody could hit Ryan, and Singer had close to unhittable stuff. I'm not taking anything away from Jeff. He was a fine major league catcher, but if Sandy

Koufax threw a no-hitter you know that Sandy Koufax is going to throw a no-hitter no matter who caught him.

– Fran Healy

Nolan Ryan, 6-0, vs. Detroit on July 15, 1973

I'd caught him plenty of times before. That particular game, the first three hitters, when I set up on the outside it was there, a hundred miles an hour. Curveball was there. Go inside. Fastball was there. You just had a sense, because he'd already thrown one against Kansas City. And that's one of those things—a catcher always wants to catch a no-hitter. So as the game was going along, he was coasting. He struck out seventeen guys, which was the most in a no-hitter. And he was just, he was right there. He was right there. Curveball and everything.

A lot of times he could beat you to death back there, but he was a real competitor. As the game went on, nobody was saying nothing, but I knew. Everybody knows.

Sometimes guys will agree with the catcher, but he was going to throw what he wanted to throw. You could be two and two, and he'd throw them a curveball. You'd be three and two, and he might want to throw a curveball even when he's throwing a hundred miles an hour. A couple of the managers would get upset. They would yell at me, and I'd say, "Look, he's going to throw what he wants to throw, and if I put it down he'll still throw what he wants to throw. I don't want to be looking curveball when he's throwing a fastball."

– Art Kusnyer

<u>Tom Seaver, 4-0, vs. St. Louis on June 16, 1978</u>

Johnny Bench went through a period where he had a bad back and couldn't play, and I played for that month of June. Pretty much that whole month I played. I caught thirty days in a row, and that just happened to be when Seaver threw it.

– *Don Werner*

Catching the Knuckler

I was catching, and Hoyt Wilhelm's relieving every damn day. He threw one you could catch, and then when you had to get the out he threw one where you'd just have to jump in front of it. That's basically what we did. He was there about half a year when Frank Lane came on as the general manager. He replaced Hank Greenberg. Lane traded Wilhelm to Baltimore. So Paul Richards, at Baltimore, when he got him over there—[Gus] Triandos was the catcher at Baltimore—well, that's when he made that big fricking glove. It still didn't help much. Gus set a record, I think, for passed balls. That was the happiest moment of my life to get rid of that son of a bitch. I mean, he was a good friend and all of that. Joe Gordon was the manager and Joe tried everything. He put J.W. Porter behind the plate one night to catch with a first baseman's glove.

– *Russ Nixon*

When Hoyt and I were with Baltimore, Paul Richards who was the manager, he was a catcher, and he said,

"Keep your eyes above the ball. Never let the ball get above your eyes. That way you can always stay in front of the ball. And while you're in front of it, if you don't happen to catch it, it'll hit you somewhere and it won't go by you." And that sort of helped. You had to battle him, though. It wasn't easy. You just had to battle him.

They called it the elephant glove, and I have a picture of Hoyt and myself looking at the glove. It really helped, because it was big and you could catch the knuckleball. The only trouble with it was if there was a man on first, and you did catch the ball, the glove was so big that the ball was in there but you couldn't get a hold of it as quickly as you wanted to.

There were other knuckleball pitchers in the league, but never one whose ball broke as much as Wilhelm's did. He had the best I've ever seen, and I think he's got the best one that ever was.

One time Mickey Mantle had just come up to the plate for the first time, and Wilhelm threw him that knuckleball. Mickey swung as hard as he could, and he must've missed it a mile. He said to me, "How far did I miss that ball?" And I said, "Mickey, you missed it farther than I missed it."

–Joe Ginsberg

A knuckleballer is tough to catch because the ball is unpredictable. It can do things that you wouldn't believe a knuckleball can do, or any kind of a pitch can do. Gus Triandos, who caught Hoyt Wilhelm for a couple of years when Wilhelm was a starting pitcher, did a marvelous job catching them, but he broke the league record for passed balls. If you look at the stats, that wouldn't look very good.

– *Red Wilson*

I've caught guys that weren't strictly knuckleball pitchers but had knuckleballs. That's one pitch, right there, that'll teach you to let the ball come to you. Because that's one pitch that if you extend to catch it, you ain't going to catch it.

I think it might be a good tool to learn to let the ball get to you, as opposed to extending and catching. You'll chase balls all night long if you don't do that. The problem is there aren't enough good ones around to throw it.

– *Mike O'Berry*

You've got to wait until it comes to you. Sometimes you get anxious and you kind of reach for it or something, and that's when you get into trouble. You don't want to be stabbing at it. When you call for a curveball or breaking ball of some kind, in your mind you know the ball's going to be breaking, and you prepare yourself because the ball's going to break that way. You're not going to wait until the last second. You know in your mind –what we call a mental shift—that the ball is going to be breaking. The right-hander's is going to break down and away from you, or from the hitter, so you prepare yourself to go that way. With the knuckleball you know it's going to be breaking, so you have to prepare yourself. Mostly I learned that it was breaking down, and so I'd go with it that way.

– *Andy Seminick*

Dutch Leonard's knuckleball: it broke down, sometimes it broke in, sometimes it broke up. He had one of the great knuckleballs. He was one of the great knuckleball pitchers of his time.

– *Andy Seminick*

Knuckleballers, I'm telling you, they destroyed me. I went to Kansas City and I was a good receiver. I knew that, and I don't mind bragging. I could catch. And I went over there, and all four of my starters were knuckleballers, and the first man out of the bullpen was a knuckleballer. When I left there at the end of two years I was a lousy receiver. Mentally it'll kill you. I don't care what anybody says. I think somebody asked Bob Uecker, "How do you catch a knuckleball?" He said, "Wait'll it stops rolling."

Ray Boone, he came over with us, and he said, I don't understand how you can sit back there with them guys on third and everything, and just throw knuckleball, knuckleball. I said, "The only chance the guy's got to get somebody out is to throw the knuckleball. And it's my job to try to at least block it." But it mentally destroyed me because, like I said, there wasn't any reprieve. Every day you went out there it was knuckleballers. It was horrible.

I didn't even have the mental approach when I left

there. Because normally you do things without thinking, but after two years of that, mentally I was not there anymore when it came to catching.

– *Frank House*

You know, Mickey Mantle had a good knuckleball. He used to throw it along the sidelines all the time just to kind of make his teammates look bad trying to catch it. But it's one thing throwing it on the side and getting it over the plate on a regular basis.

– *Red Wilson*

Injuries

I still play a lot of golf. I go to the Bob Hope in January. That helps. Al Lopez, he's got the two bad knees. He can't play golf. He says, "Keep playing golf, Yogi. Keep playing. Best thing for you."

– *Yogi Berra*

Knees, achy knees. I've had six knee surgeries now. Only two when I played. I think the worst thing about catching was after I got done playing my knees just keep disintegrating. The cartilage in there just keeps tearing every few years. The cartilage in there is just frayed, and they clean it up and they cut it out and it's smooth again, then you try to run, ride a bike, go skiing. You do different things to try and stay active, and they tend to keep going again. Modern medicine is just so good that the knee surgeries aren't anything like they used to be. Heck, you're walking in two or three days, and you're back on a bicycle in two weeks.

– *Bob Geren*

I've still got neck problems now with these top couple of vertebrae keep getting out of line. The lower back pain that I have, I know that's from catching. I never really had any knee problems, but your hamstrings just stay so tight all the time, and that pulls on the sciatic nerve. I've always had some lower back pain that's bothered me through the years. But I've been very fortunate knee-wise.

– *Mike O'Berry*

I sprained my ankles doing blocking drills, just because I didn't know how to properly get down in position to block a ball in the dirt. I had somebody run me over in Single A, and I ran to the wrong dugout after the collision. They had to come get me because I was out of it. I was in the wrong position, probably because I still didn't know how to block the plate. I've had my finger broken from a Sammy Sosa foul tip. That set me back. You know, last year I had my neck swung around on a foul tip. I'm just trying to think of all of them.

– *Keith Osik*

Yeah, you get run over. I was fortunate enough, that in all my career—it was fourteen years—I never got a finger broken by a foul tip. The only finger I had broken was when Harmon Killebrew stepped on my opposite hand

and broke my middle finger. I don't know. I guess I was just lucky. I had foul tips hit my right hand, but I think maybe I kept my hand relaxed, and maybe the fingers turned down a little bit, is the reason I didn't get any broken fingers.

But you get run over. Lord have mercy, I was run over so many times I can't count them. And I'm paying for that now. Nowadays, at my age, all the areas that I got hurt when I was young—I didn't think anything about it—but now they come back to haunt you.

– Frank House

I guess the worst one I had was a dislocated hip in Pittsburgh one day. I had three plays at home plate in the same inning—Dick Groat, Joel Skinner and Joe Christopher. Christopher came headfirst and hit me up around my right thigh. My left side was on the plate, you know, and his head got inside on my thigh. His body got inside on my right thigh and dislocated my hip. That's the only time I ever took myself out of a ballgame.

I was going to play the second game of the doubleheader and I told Alvin [Dark], "I cannot go. I'm sorry to tell you that." So they had Dr. Goldstein or something like that, in Pittsburgh—he was an old-timer around there—he came in and he said, "He'll be okay." Well, that night I couldn't even get off the airplane in Chicago, and I called our trainer. I said, "Doc, I've got to have some help." The next morning we go over to the hospital, and the guy pulled that leg, and it sounded like a cap gun going off when it went back in there. Pow! Just the suction in the thing. I had a couple days in the whirlpool and was ready to go again.

– *Ed Bailey*

I think my worst collision, that I felt the most in the big leagues, was with Phil Nevin. He got me. He was tagging up at third. It was a fly ball to [Larry] Walker in right and he threw a perfect one-hop throw home and I caught it and right as I caught it he got me. I got up and I was fine—I played the rest of the game and everything—but the next day I remember having whiplash and feeling that one pretty good.

– *Ben Petrick*

Three years ago I had surgery on my right knee. I had a torn meniscus and I had surgery. That same year I'd gotten released by the Marlins. I went home for a month and Oakland called me and they sent me to Double A. I just went, "Wow. I'm thirty-one and going back to Double A." That was tough, especially after tasting the big leagues in '97. You do what you want to do, but at the bottom you've got to ask yourself, "Do you still love the game?" And I said, "I do."

– *Mandy Romero*

The Catcher's Nature

I think most catchers, by nature, like to be in charge. They enjoy the challenge of running the game. They want to be involved in every play. I played in the outfield sometimes, and it was horrible. You just stand out there, inning after inning, and nothing ever happens. I was used to, before every play started, I had something to do with it. I started the play by giving the sign. Catchers like to be involved.

Most of them like the challenge of running the game, and calling the pitches, and trying to beat the hitter and beat the baserunners, the pitch out, setting up the defenses. They really like that. Most of them, after baseball, are in charge of something—either their own business or they're running businesses for someone else. Many of them, as you know, go back into baseball or remain in baseball and become pretty successful big league managers.

– *Mike Compton*

For some reason, I don't know, maybe the catcher just likes the game a little more, gets a little bit more into the intricacies and mindset of the game, and is not just going out there playing. Catchers appreciate the little things in the game more than other guys do. It's a little bit of a chess match. You definitely have to be a thinking man to be a good catcher.

– *Tim Laker*

In a catcher I want somebody to take charge. Your job as a catcher is to be as honest as you can with the pitcher and the manager. Not the pitching coach but the manager, because he's the one you have to answer to. And the pitcher's the one that's out there. So when you go out there you're in charge. I'm looking for someone that has a big heart and guts. Intestinal fortitude.

– Elrod Hendricks

I played for Jim Riggleman in A ball when he was twenty-six years old. It was about my third year of pro ball. I liked the lifestyle, you know. I like going city to city and traveling, and not having to do homework. I never felt like baseball was a real job. I'm not saying it because I'm lazy or anything. It's work. I always worked to win. But I always felt like, What a job, you know? I can't believe you get paid for this. When I saw him as a young manager and stuff, I was learning the game. I thought I had a pretty good feel for the game, being a catcher. And he would sit, a lot of times, next to me on the bus. He'd say something like, "Do you know why I brought that lefthander in there to face that guy?" And I'd say, "No."

I'd learn different things from different managers. And I found myself managing, doing the same thing. I'd be on the bench, and sometimes you're worked up by the situation, and you want to talk. You say something like, "Can you believe they're not pinch-hitting him right here? I would. Because look, I have nobody to face him. My guy pitched three innings last night in the bullpen. They should probably pinch-hit this guy. I hope they don't." And you teach guys all the time. Or you see a baserunning mistake by the other team. I'd say, "There's no outs there. He's got to tag up. His job's not to score, it's to get to third. Wouldn't it be amazing if we won this game by one run and it's because of that?" You're always talking to your players, and I've had managers that would do that, and you'd soak it in.

I felt like I always sat right behind the manager on the bus for a couple of reasons. You wanted to learn all you could, and you also wanted to stay away from the guys in the back that wanted to drink and mess around and play cards. I wanted to sleep because I was tired, being a catcher, so I would always gravitate towards the front of the bus for numerous reasons.

Another benefit was being close to the manager and listening to him talk to his coach about stuff, and sometimes just listening to what's going on. It's kind of nice to be in the know of what's going on with the team. You don't know what you can learn. You never know.

– Bob Geren

A good catcher is a guy who's willing to figure out a way to get it done, a guy that wants to be able to stay in the major leagues no matter how hard it's going to be or what he's got to do, a guy that's there mentally every single day. As a coach I'm not looking for the rah-rah college guy. I'm just looking for a guy who pays attention, who's not afraid to make a decision and live with it. I could look at a couple of guys and say, "He's an athlete. He's not an everyday player."

– Jamie Quirk

Career Highlights

We were playing at the end of the season. We'd been in first place for about the last half of the season and we'd gone on a road trip, and it was kind of an extended road trip to the best of my memory. But I hadn't played in two weeks. It might've been three weeks, I don't know. I just wasn't playing. I brought a couple of bats to take batting practice with and ended up breaking both of them. We were playing the last day in Boston. We were tied 3-3 in the seventh inning. If we won that would give us a three-game lead with four to play. Baltimore had tore us up all year, so we really needed to win this game and I was in the bullpen.

I remember the bullpen phone rang. I grabbed my glove to warm up a pitcher, but Ted Simmons had just got a hit, and they had to pinch-run for him and they called down and said that I was going to catch. I saw the score was 3-3, got loose, ran in. Caught the bottom of the seventh, caught the bottom of the eighth, and in the top of the ninth inning—I just remember the score was still tied 3-3—and I was the fifth hitter. I was thinking to myself, What am I going to do for a bat if I get up? Hopefully we can score before I get up. So I'm fumbling around looking for a bat. I ran to the clubhouse, and I'm looking for a bat, and finally I grabbed one of Charlie Moore's bats and ran back down.

Jim Gantner led off and made an out. Paul Molitor got up next and got a base hit. And Robin Yount was up and the count got to two and two. Molly stole second,

Robin struck out. So it's two outs, runner on second, a tie ballgame, Cecil Cooper's on deck and I'm hitting right behind Cecil. They called timeout, manager walked out and they're looking at me and Cooper, and to this point I'm still trying to get my shin guards off, and I'd just found a bat, still really not knowing what's going on. They walk back and then they intentionally walk Cooper. That's when I first said, "Oh, dang."

Now it's two outs, runners on first and second, and here I haven't played in three weeks. And what I was trying to do was just hit a blooper over the second baseman's head to try to score the run. You got Mark Clear out there, and at that time he was one of the best relievers in the American League. The first pitch he threw me was a curveball that broke about nine feet. I don't know how—it was right down the middle—but the umpire called it ball one. I remember stepping out and the crowd was booing, and I was thinking to myself, Man, I am in trouble with this dude here.

The next pitch he threw me a fastball kind of right down the middle, and in your whole life, every time you hit a home run you know. You just know that feeling, right? Well, I hit this ball, and as soon as I hit it I saw out of the corner of my eye Jim Rice turn, in Boston, and start running back to the wall. Well, I was just praying that he wouldn't catch it. And that ball went so far into the net. I think it might've gone over the net, that's how far I hit it, but my first instinct was, Don't catch it. Don't catch it. When the ball went over I just remember sprinting around the bases, back to the dugout, and it was a total mob scene there. Here we are winning, 6-3, and everybody knew how big this game was and how much we needed to win it.

The dugouts were very small in Boston, and by the time we kind of got settled down and after all the commotion, you could hear, "Hey, hey." Harvey Kuenn had fallen down between the bench and the bat rack, and they had to pull him up. You know, everybody had backed him down into the corner. But we ended up winning that ballgame, went into Baltimore with a three-game lead, and just got killed in a doubleheader Friday night and then got killed on Saturday, and we came down to the last day of the year tied and ended up winning that ballgame, so it was a big home run.

It was the only real highlight of my career.

– *Ned Yost*

We won the World Series in '95. That was a big experience. It took me one month to get a ring. Guys play for fifteen, sixteen years and they don't have a ring. It took me one month to get one. But I spent eight years in the minor leagues.

– *Eddie Perez*

I think the best day of my career was Opening Day in St. Louis. We opened up in Montreal—it was freezing—but when we got to St. Louis [Bob] Gibson was pitching. I warmed him up, and they stopped for the National

Anthem, and I took a look and said, "My God, this is really happening?" I mean, thirty, forty, fifty thousand people, and I'm on the other side not paying. And that was probably when it really got to me that I had really got there. All the hard work and everything else paid off.

– *Bart Zeller*

I hear this a lot and I agree—the first time you put on a major league uniform, it's kind of an awesome thing. I faced Denny McLain my first major league at-bat, and he won thirty games the year before, and I think he won twenty-five or twenty-six that year. I remember getting one, maybe two hits in that game off of Denny McLain. I know I got my first hit off him in Kansas City at the old ballpark. It's a fascinating experience. You know, you're percolating through all those years of baseball and all of a sudden, bang, it's ready. The coffee's ready the day you go on the field your first major league game because you've made it, even if it's for a day.

– *Fran Healy*

The End of the Career

It was a relief for me. My wife was a mess. She cried the whole time. But it was a relief for me. Being on the other end of it, as a coach, at times you have to release players and that's not fun. You see some players that really show emotions. Others don't. And that's why I always said to myself, I'm always going to tell the truth. I'm never going to say, "This was a numbers game." How many times have you heard that? No, it wasn't a numbers game. You weren't playing well. You hear it all the time—"You got caught up in the numbers." If you play good enough, you're not going to get caught up in the numbers.

–*John Tamargo*

Baseball has always been something that I've liked. Even when I wasn't playing as a kid I was watching it. I just liked the game, and when I got out of baseball in '85, I really didn't want anything to do with it.

I remember when Harry Walker was at UAB, and I'd come back in the winter, I'd work out over there with them, and he used to tell me, "You think you've got all your friends now. Wait until you get out of the game. The ones who are still playing won't know who you are." And that's sort of true. While you're playing you all keep in touch, but once you get out, they've got their own group. It's kind of funny how that kind of circle runs.

When I got released by the Yankees that year, I had a minor league contract for seventy thousand dollars, and when they tell you they're going to release you because George don't want to pay a minor league veteran you kind of wonder what's going on with that. Anyway, I got picked up by Montreal and finished the season that year, and I think I did okay when I was up there. Murray Cook was the GM at that time, and I can't remember if he was with the Yankees or the Reds when I was with that particular club, but I was talking to him at the end of the year, and he was telling me how surprised he was with how well I threw, and I said, "Well damn, Murray, how in the hell do you think I got here?"

But I go home and they call and they want to give me a minor league contract again. At that point in time you're really kind of tired of two months here, two months there, two months here, two months there. So I said, "Let me think about it." I had a couple of offers there and even the next year, but it was just to the point, at that particular time, Do I want to go up and down, up and down, up and down? Hindsight's always 20/20. I probably wish I'd said, Okay, just hang on. But when you have family and all that type stuff, a lot of things come into play when you're thirty-two or thirty-three years old. At some point you've just got to say, I got to give it up. So I just got out completely, and for about a year or so I didn't do anything with baseball.

– *Mike O'Berry*

Today's Catcher

More and more in Little League, in high school and even in college, they're taking away authority and responsibility from the catcher. Managers and coaches want to show their authority by calling pitches and all of that, so the kids never develop. A lot of them are turned off because of it.

When they get to the pros, they haven't been able to use their mentality to catch. You see the College World Series, the Little League World Series. They're looking in the dugout for signs. That has taken away from the development of the catcher. They get into the pros and all of a sudden you're relying on them to call the ballgame, and you realize this guy has no clue what he's doing. The only way he can learn is by going out there.

– Elrod Hendricks

Piazza's in a league of his own with that bat. He's not only a great hitting catcher, he's a great right-handed hitter. When you have a Piazza, you're going to find a place for him to play. His throwing has been bad the past couple of years, but he still has decent velocity so basically, to me, it's confidence. He's lost his confidence, which happens.

What do you do? Do you take a guy out of the lineup that can't throw but can drive in 110 runs because he's not throwing out guys at second? How important is the stolen base? To me it was important that I throw a guy out. It bothered me. It bothers him. If you're the manager, he's so valuable you've got to get that off his mind. He does a nice job receiving the ball, calling the game. Calling the game's like poetry. It means one thing to you, it means another thing to me.

– Fran Healy

I'll tell you what, I see some catchers today that are terrible, terrible receivers. I mean, you can help the pitcher so much if you can take the low ball and catch it up, but they go out there on the low ball and they're slapping it down and taking it further and further out of the strike zone. The umpires are not going to give you a strike on that. I think that's so important, that you try to bring the ball into the strike zone. Not so obvious that everybody knows what you're doing, because the umpires are not dummies.

– *Frank House*

To be honest, I think there are some catchers in today's game that just want to hit, and they catch because that's their position. That pride in handling the defensive responsibilities has slipped to some degree. Part of that's due to the nature of the game now. You could be the greatest handler of pitchers in the world, but if you hit .220 you might be out of a job.

– *Bob Geren*

The major league temperament—I guess you'd call it temperament—is different today. I hadn't been back in the big leagues until two years ago when I went back with Pittsburgh. I'd been with Cincinnati and San Diego, as a Triple A manager, coordinator, farm guy, so I'd been away from the big league clubhouse for about ten years. It shocked me because nobody hung out with anybody. When I was with Cleveland—that was a veteran ballclub—and when the game was over there was always four cases of beer iced down in the middle of the clubhouse, and nobody left until it was done. We'd sit there and bullshit about the game.

Today, before I get in off the field, most of the players are in the shower, and half of them are gone. So the game is not talked about at all. And there's no way in hell that the manager is going to be able to say, "Stay here and talk about the game." Unless he has called a meeting, he's not going to do that. You've got single rooms. You don't have to deal with another guy. You're on your own. Some of them don't even want anybody near them. It's altogether a different atmosphere out there now, a different make-up. You look for a team concept, but there's not a team concept.

– *Russ Nixon*

I've always said that if a catcher can be a good effective, defensive catcher in A ball, it's a piece of cake for him to catch in the major leagues. In A ball you can slip low and outside and they may fire it up and in, and they're firing it hard. It's much more difficult to do the physical tasks of catching at those levels. Most of those major league pitchers, they pretty well throw the ball where they want to.

– *Mike Compton*

Today I watch guys and all the catchers—not all of them but 90 percent of them—they slap down on the ball. You've got to keep the palm up. Anything above your belt has to be palm down. Anything up to your belt ought to be palms up, particularly the low pitch. You're pushing the ball back towards the mound, keeping the thing in front of you, and these guys are slapping down and backhanding. Lopez in Atlanta is a good catcher—I'm not knocking the guy—but he catches the ball so bad sometimes. He takes the pitch away from some of those guys because the umpire sees him slap down on it. You can kind of handle an umpire by your hands. I tried to keep my hands out front, fairly far out, and bring the ball to me all the time, bring it a little bit to me. You never have to bring it in all the way.

–*Ed Bailey*

8TH

The Battery

One of the most mysterious moments in a game for baseball fans is the meeting on the mound, when the catcher trots out to offer advice or encouragement to the pitcher. Fans can only imagine what's being said. Now that we live in a time when most games are televised, the catcher and pitcher add to the mystery by speaking to each other through their gloves, so that opposing snoops can't read their lips, deduce the strategy the battery mates are concocting, and then somehow relay this precious cargo of information to the batter standing at home plate.

Sometimes the catcher says little more than "Go get 'em," his visit merely a way of helping his pitcher regain rhythm or giving him a minute to collect his thoughts. Other times the two review the plan discussed at the pregame meeting for getting the hitter out, a restatement of the hitter's weaknesses and tendencies. As should be obvious, pitching is a collaborative effort, one in which the catcher plays a crucial role, if one not always apparent to the casual fan.

Some batteries develop a close bond, even to the point at which a pitcher insists on being caught only by one catcher. More than a few weak-hitting backstops have extended their careers by being the choice of a good pitcher. Catchers have various opinions on the battery relationship, and on the role each man plays.

Working with Pitchers

I don't recall any pitchers that I really disliked. Whether you go out to dinner that night, or you're the type of guy that calls during the winter to say "Merry Christmas," I don't think that matters. If you're constantly bickering and fighting, you don't like the way he treats you professionally, where every time he gives up a hit he comes in and blames you for it, that could be a nightmare, but I've never experienced that. I've seen pitchers do that to catchers, which I didn't think was fair, because ultimately, when you talk about game-calling, they have the final say on every team I've been on. I've never been on a team where they say, "The catcher calls the game and you throw it, period." I'm sure there have been some situations where, you know, Carlton Fisk is in the league eighteen years and a rookie comes up from Triple A and the pitching coach says, "Throw everything Pudge says." I'm sure there are situations like that occasionally, but in general that doesn't happen.

– *Bob Geren*

Sometimes you need to put your arm around them. Other times you need to kick them in the butt. You have to know your personnel. If you have to use strong language to a guy, do it. But there's some guys you can't do that with. You can't say anything harsh to them because you'll lose them. So you have to know the personnel. You have to know the whole staff better than they know themselves.

– *Elrod Hendricks*

I think that the pitching staff has to have confidence in a catcher. The pitching staff is not going to be able to throw good breaking balls, or good sliders, things of that kind, where they need to be thrown if they have some doubt that it's not going to wind up at the backstop. So you have to be good at that. You have to instill in the pitching staff, "Don't you worry about it." You throw it where you're supposed to throw it. It's my responsibility to make sure that it stays out in front of the plate.

I really think that concentrating on working with the pitcher, knowing the pitcher, understanding the pitcher, is really as important, or more important, than the offensive production. I think that should be first in your mind, and then, offensively, of course, you hope to contribute too.

There are certain things that a catcher should absolutely know. Number one, in my mind, the catcher knows better how the pitcher's throwing than anyone else. I don't care—pitching coaches, managers—the guy sitting behind the plate should know, and probably will know, whether the guy is throwing good or not. That's the reason you see—at least during my career—when the pitching coach or the manager goes to the mound, the catcher goes too. There was always a conversation between the pitching coach and me. What do you think? How's he throwing? The catcher has to keep this in mind when he's back there working. He's got to know the pitcher's best pitch, and always, always remember that if you're going to get beat, get beat with your best pitch. Period. All the rest of the stuff, you know, is minor compared to that. We're going to go with your best pitch, and if we're going to lose it we're going to lose it with that, and not some off-speed thing.

That happened with Billy Hoeft. It was the last day of the 1956 season. [Tigers manager] Bucky Harris pitched him maybe a day earlier or something. When you have nineteen wins, everybody wants to get twenty, so Hoeft was trying to get it. We've got a good lead, and he ain't ever thrown a knuckleball in his life. I called something, and here comes the damn knuckleball. I started out to the mound. He thought it was funny. I said, "Hoeft, you dumb blankety-blank. Everybody out here is working their butts off to help you get this twentieth win, and you're out here screwing around." I said, "Now that's it. No more of that crap." Well, the smile left his face. We went on, and he won the ballgame, but that's kind of what I'm talking about right there.

– *Frank House*

Early in the game you don't want to catch a pitcher into trouble. In other words, you're not going to gamble on 3-2 with nobody on in the first or second inning. You're not going to get the pitcher into trouble where he'll be too fine. Give him a little freedom and let them hit the ball. Just throw strikes instead of pinpointing the ball on the corner on 3-2 in the first and second inning. All of a sudden you're walking somebody, and somebody boots the ball, and a guy hits a home run, and now you're down three to nothing. Early in the game is what I stress a lot to the young catchers. Don't catch a pitcher into trouble.

– *Andy Seminick*

I was not a psychology major in school or anything, but I think that that plays a big role in how your pitcher performs. What you say to him and when and why and how. You learn that, really, through trial and error. Nobody sits you down and teaches you how to do it. But you hear different things. That's how you learn. You hear things like, "When you go to the mound with this guy, don't throw any negatives in his head. Be positive." Or, "When you go to this guy you might have to kick him in gear. He's a little bit lackadaisical." Or, "When you go to the mound, use a calm voice because this guy's so excited out there. Your job is to calm him down." But then the majority of it you kind of learn on your own. You have to know the guy.

I look back on the friendships I had when I was playing, and I always seemed to hang out with the pitchers. If they were going to go get a beer, I'd go with them. Or if I'd call somebody and say, "Hey, you want to go get breakfast," it always seemed like it was a pitcher. I never consciously made an effort to do it. It just happened. I never thought about it until I looked back on it.

– *Bob Geren*

When the pitcher throws strikes, it makes the catcher look good. When the pitcher throws in the dirt and around and up and down, that makes the catcher look bad.

– *Joe Ginsberg*

You owe it to your teammates, you owe it to your management, and you owe it to the pitcher to be honest. You don't do him any good if you're protecting him, because if his arm is getting tired, and he's lost a lot off his ball, unless he's just lucky, he's not going to come out of it too well, especially if he's in a situation with men on base and the middle of that order coming up. You're not going to do him any good by saying, "Oh yeah, he can get through this," when he's really lost a lot off his stuff.

As a catcher, you have a pretty good feel for that. You see the arm slot pretty well too. A lot of pitchers, as that shoulder gets tired, don't realize it but that arm is not riding as high through the throwing area as it was when it was fresh. And they don't know that. The arm is kind of like a sprinter, a quarter-miler. He's coming down the last one hundred meters, and the coaches are trying to get him to lift those legs, because the fatigued muscles are just not picking them up. It's the same thing with throwing. That arm is riding a little lower and he's starting to push the ball up a little bit. You've been watching that arm slot all day long. If you're paying any attention you can see that he's not right up there, and the ball is losing some of its impact. It's riding up a little bit. If you're doing your due diligence back there, and you're really a catcher, then you pick up on that stuff.

– *Mike Compton*

Battery Mates

Ewell Blackwell

Ewell Blackwell was tough. Sometimes his stuff was so good he couldn't throw strikes. He'd throw it right down the middle and it'd move so much it'd be off the plate. But he was a tough pitcher. You get in a close game and you just start having him throw his best stuff and hope it's a strike, hope it's over the plate, which most of the time it was. He threw a fastball, curveball and he had a knock-down pitch too. He was tough. He was mean with it.

– *Andy Seminick*

Jim Bunning

When I first started catching Jim, I thought that he would probably shake off every pitch, like, "Hey, I'm going to call my own game for this guy." But surprisingly he either thought I knew what I was doing or just thought the protocol is for the catcher to call the game, because for the most part he would work with me. He didn't shake me off too much at all. Of course, he had two pitches. That helped. It wasn't like he had four pitches, and you're trying to work with them.

I always liked working with Jim. He never made me feel like I was a rookie, and he was somebody else. He was a perfect gentleman. I'm not surprised that Jim is where he is today, because he always had that quality about him when you're on the team with him. He was dignified even then. If I remember right, he even helped negotiate some of the younger players' contracts back then. Even as a player, he kind of represented them. He was getting started in those kinds of roles even back then. He was a fine person.

– *Mike Compton*

Steve Busby

I'll tell you a thing about Busby. He threw a no-hitter in Detroit. We came to New York to the old Yankee Stadium to play the Yankees and Jack McKeon held him out because he thought the media would be harsh. Compared to today it's nothing. We went to Milwaukee after that, if memory serves me correct, and he threw five or six no-hit innings in Milwaukee and then someone, George Scott I think, got a hit. He was throwing no-hitters back to back. Then the following year he did throw a no-hitter against Milwaukee.

Basically, late in the game, when the guy's throwing a

no-hitter, you're hoping that the ball will be hit at somebody. Probably the guy out there is going, "Shit, don't hit it to me." But as a catcher you're hoping the ball will be hit at somebody, or he'll strike somebody out. I can only imagine what's going through their body in the infield and the outfield.

In my opinion, if anybody would've beat Nolan Ryan as far as no-hitters were concerned, Busby would've if he had stayed healthy. Busby had no-hit stuff when he went on the mound, when he was healthy. He had a real good fastball. It was heavy. And he had a nasty breaking ball. And when he got on the mound, he thought he was going to throw a no-hitter.

He hurt his arm his third year in the big leagues. A lot of people don't realize that. Reggie Jackson told me he couldn't hit him. George Hendrick had trouble with Busby too. I'll never forget one time he decided to hang in there after trying to hit Busby's breaking ball. Busby threw him that hard, heavy fastball and broke Hendrick's wrist. Lou Pinella, good major league hitter, had trouble with Busby. If Busby did what he did in New York they'd be writing sonnets about him.

– *Fran Healy*

Mike Cuellar

We were roommates, and we talked an awful lot. A lot of times we'd talk about the game before the game. I mean, two days before he pitched sometimes we'd go over the other ballclub. We knew who was swinging the bat well and we'd talk about who we wanted to pitch around in certain situations. If Earl [Weaver] doesn't put him on, we'll do this. We'll pitch around and get the next guy, and this is the way we want to attack this next guy. We went over the game and talked about it.

– Elrod Hendricks

Ned Garver

One of the toughest guys to catch was Ned Garver. He was a great pitcher for the Browns, and I caught him for years, and he never threw anything I called.

I mean, never.

If you stop to think about it, the reason that it's so difficult is that you get into a mind set. All right, I called the slider, it's going to be a slider. But if you change your thinking—I've called a slider but he may throw anything—then you do different things. So I made up my mind. I say I made up my mind, but he made it up for me. I said, "Okay, I'm giving him a sign, but he was always a thinker, and he'd get into his windup and maybe he'd say, "I'm not going to throw the slider. I'm going to throw this fastball." Of course that scenario, going from a breaking ball to a fastball, was much tougher on me because I don't have as much time to react.

– Frank House

Steve Gromek

Steve Gromek, now, you knew he wasn't going to blow the ball by anybody, but when Steve Gromek was right the game lasted an hour and forty-five minutes. There was eighteen pop-ups to the infield, no walks, and he had nothing but a fastball. If he tried to throw a breaking ball he'd usually hit the hitter with it.

– Frank House

Ken Holtzman

He was his own man. I caught him in Toronto, and I think he won 1-0 on a Sunday. A week goes by. The following Sunday we're back in New York at the Stadium. Detroit's in town. And everything they're hitting is up. End of the bat, he's breaking the bat. Nobody's hitting the ball hard, but balls are dropping in. There were two outs, and Billy Martin's pissed off. Martin loved the breaking ball.

Holtzman, by the way, didn't throw his breaking ball. For some reason he stopped throwing it, but he had great control of a good fastball. He didn't overcomplicate the thing. So Martin goes out to the mound and says, "I want you to throw all curveballs the rest of the game." He's walking to the dugout, his back is to us, and I'm giving the sign fastball, bang, third out. Martin's back is to the field. Fastball. Third out. Holtzman is in the dugout, and rather than arguing with him, he says, "My arm's sore. I'm going home." Up the runway he goes and went home.

– Fran Healy

Greg Maddux

Maddux likes to have somebody who'll take care of him, who'll talk about the game with him, so the regular catcher won't be doing that because he'll be playing, but Maddux likes his catcher to sit with him.

He loves communication, so we'd talk about the game before the game, what we're going to do, game situations, and all that stuff. And with the everyday catcher it's going to be hard to do that stuff.

He wanted me to think his way, and he wanted me to do exactly what he wanted to do. He wanted to do the right thing at the right time.

The first couple of years were tough. The first game was tough because he thinks differently from everybody. He's not a normal pitcher, first of all, because of the pitches that he throws. The regular pitchers throw in this place. He's throwing to a different place, but that's the way he thinks. The first couple of years were tough because I wanted him to pitch like a regular guy, and he's not like that, but then we just got along together. We were talking all the time. We'd talk about the game, about the hitters, things like reminding each other what the hitter did in the past.

He's got a good arm. His ball moves a lot, but the thing about him is he knows a lot about hitting. He knows what the hitter's going to wait for. He knows as soon as the hitter steps in the box. He knows about hitting. Every time a player steps into the box, he knows what they're going do. He knows the pitch you throw to get him out, and he knows the pitch they're waiting for. I think he reads their minds. It's unbelievable.

– Eddie Perez

Juan Marichal

With the Giants I caught Juan Marichal and Gaylord Perry, and they had good fastballs, good movement on their fastballs. Marichal might be the most underrated pitcher in the Hall of Fame. And he would stay with his catcher. He would fill the pitch. Now, if he didn't like it, he would talk to you for three innings, but he was a great pitcher. He had great control.

You know, he was a sidearm pitcher when he was in the minor leagues. A manager named Andy Gilbert told him in Springfield, Massachusetts, that if he continued to throw sidearm he wouldn't be able to get left-handers out as well as you should. Marichal said, "Can you teach me how to throw overhand?" And Andy said, "Yes." He took him to the bullpen, and the only way he could throw overhand is he had to have that high leg kick.

– Fran Healy

Jim Palmer

Jim Palmer has not forgotten a base hit that he gave up any time in his career, and I learned an awful lot from catching him. Early in my career he was not a veteran, but he knew enough about the hitters and how he pitched them and how to get them out, so if there was a situation that came up and I need some information on a certain hitter I didn't mind going to Jim at all because I knew he would remember exactly how to throw him and how to get him out. It was no embarrassment for me to go and ask him.

He also was the most difficult pitcher for me to catch because of his knowledge. He knew himself better than anyone ever did. He knew the hitters. He remembered what they did, what they hit against him ten years before. And there were days he didn't have the stuff. We were pretty good together as far as clicking, knowing each other's strengths. I knew what he liked to go to when he got in trouble, but sometimes we'd have problems with that on days he didn't have his good stuff. And I was trying to create stuff, invent stuff for him, but he had too much pride to give in. So that's what made it tough.

– *Elrod Hendricks*

Robin Roberts

Robin Roberts, you know, had a lot of home runs hit off of him, but he won a lot of ballgames too. Robin either wanted to get you on or off on three pitches. If he had two strikes on you, you better get ready because here comes the boss. That's the way he pitched.

– *Ed Bailey*

Schoolboy Rowe

I loved catching Schoolboy Rowe. He had good control and he knew how to pitch. By catching him I learned a lot about how to call pitches.

– *Andy Seminick*

Tom Seaver

Seaver was a very unique pitcher in that he never wanted the catcher to move. You never moved on the corners. He would shoot to areas, whether it be your right shinguard, or maybe the umpire's mask, if he was coming up and in. He would shoot for targets on your body, but you always stayed in the middle. The only hard part was when you called a fastball 0 and 2, you didn't know if he was going to blow one about ninety-eight a few inches outside or whether it was going to be up and in, so you really had to be ready to go, and that was the only problem with catching him.

– *Don Werner*

Tracy Stallard

Tracy had a real good fastball and a big breaking ball. Boston was starved for pitching in [the early 60s], especially after Tom Brewer and Frank Sullivan and all those guys left. Don Schwall came in, and Tracy was part of that team. They brought all those kids in the year after I got traded over there, so all that transition was going on. The older guys were leaving , but they had those kids at Double A, and they started bringing them all in. Tracy was one of them. Tracy had good stuff, but Tracy was a bit of a character. Boston was made up of party guys, and Tracy fit right in.

– *Russ Nixon*

Dizzy Trout

I was still a fresh rookie. We played in Washington. Sam Mele batting. Trout's a big guy, strong, throwing hard sliders, and it was three and two with the winning run on third, and I called for the fastball, the sinking fastball, and he threw the biggest slider you've ever seen. He struck Mele out, and as we were walking off the field I was shaking. I mean, I caught it, but how I caught it I don't know. He put his arm around me, and he said, "Kid, you're the only catcher I would've done that with. I knew you'd catch it." I said, "Are you crazy, man?" But he had some confidence in me.

– *Frank House*

Virgil Trucks

I saw him pitch his first game. Against the St. Louis Browns. He was wild as heck, but he could throw. I was young, sixteen or seventeen. I'd go to a lot of games growing up—the Cardinal games and the Browns games. We used to have a knothole gang section. Sit up in the left field seats up there. We didn't go in no bleachers. Right down the leftfield line. The knothole gang section.

In '52 he pitched a no-hitter against us. I played in that game. He threw hard. We didn't have no guns, but I know he threw hard. We could see that with our eyes. And we had hard throwers too. Like Ryne Duren we had on our team. And [Allie] Reynolds and you know [Vic] Raschi was pretty good too.

He had good control when he pitched against us, the

no-hitter. When a guy's pitching a no-hitter on you, you say, "I'll get him next time," but you don't. That happens. He had control and he threw hard. But he never got the opportunity to play with a good team. You know when he pitched the two no-hitters he was five and nineteen. That was when their team was terrible. I didn't play enough with him to know him that well, you know, what pitches he threw and everything. Some of the guys that passed away now, they could tell how he did more.

– *Yogi Berra*

Hitting Against a Former Battery Mate

One seldom-discussed aspect of the relationship is coming up to bat against a former battery mate. Is it easier or more difficult to hit against someone with whom you've worked as a catcher? A couple of catchers respond:

You see the pitches from a different perspective, and when you know what's coming, nothing looks as sharp, nothing looks as crisp. It's a mental thing. When you've seen and caught the guy's breaking ball five hundred times, when you actually get to the plate and see one it's like an old friend coming at you. Definitely. I think what helped me was seeing it come out of his hands so many times I actually recognized it earlier. And a big part of hitting is pitch recognition.

Here's a good example. Calvin Schiraldi. He owned me in the 1984-85 Texas League. I couldn't get a hit off this guy. In the Texas League All-Star game I caught him for three innings. The very next time I faced him I hit a home run. I didn't think so much after that.

– Bob Geren

You know what he's going to throw you, but you know what? They probably pitch differently too, because they know my weakness. In fact, I faced [John] Smoltz the other day in Atlanta and never expected that he was going to throw me the fastball, but that's what he did. And I wasn't ready for it. He threw me three fastballs. I talked to him after the game. I said, "What are you doing? Are you crazy?" He said, "What were you looking for?" I said, "The damn slider." He said, "I know."

– Eddie Perez

9TH

The Lists

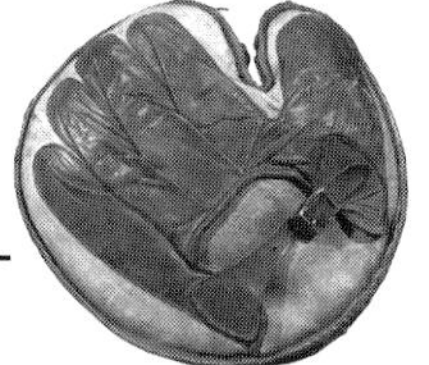

Hall of Famer RICK FERRELL blocks the New York Yankees' Hank Johnson at the plate.

Hall of Famers

Johnny Lee Bench

Bats: Right Throws: Right

Height: 6'1" Weight: 208 lbs.

Born: Dec. 7, 1947 in Oklahoma City, OK

Major League Debut: Aug. 28, 1967

Hall of Fame Inductee – 1989

YEAR	TEAM	LG	POS	G	AB	R	H	2B	3B	HR	RBI	TB	AVG	SLG
1967	Cin	NL	C	26	86	7	14	3	1	1	6	22	.163	.256
1968	Cin	NL	C	154	564	67	155	40	2	15	82	244	.275	.433
1969	Cin	NL	C	148	532	83	156	23	1	26	90	259	.293	.487
1970	Cin	NL	C	158	605	97	177	35	4	45	148	355	.293	.587
1971	Cin	NL	C	149	562	80	134	19	2	27	61	238	.238	.423
1972	Cin	NL	C	147	538	87	145	22	2	40	125	291	.270	.541
1973	Cin	NL	C	152	557	83	141	17	3	25	104	239	.253	.429
1974	Cin	NL	C	160	621	108	174	38	2	33	129	315	.280	.507
1975	Cin	NL	C	142	530	83	150	39	1	28	110	275	.283	.519
1976	Cin	NL	C	135	465	62	109	24	1	16	74	183	.234	.394
1977	Cin	NL	C	142	494	67	136	34	2	31	109	267	.275	.540
1978	Cin	NL	C	120	393	52	102	17	1	23	73	190	.260	.483
1979	Cin	NL	C	130	464	73	128	19	0	22	80	213	.276	.459
1980	Cin	NL	C	114	360	52	90	12	0	24	68	174	.250	.483
1981	Cin	NL	1B	52	178	14	55	8	0	8	25	87	.309	.489
1982	Cin	NL	3B	119	399	44	103	16	0	13	38	158	.258	.396
1983	Cin	NL	3B	110	310	32	79	15	2	12	54	134	.255	.432
TOTALS				**2158**	**7658**	**1091**	**.267**	**381**	**24**	**389**	**1376**	**3644**	**.267**	**.476**

Lawrence Peter "Yogi" Berra
Bats: Left Throws: Right
Height: 5'8" Weight: 194 lbs.
Born: May 12, 1925 in St.Louis, MO
Major League Debut: Sept. 22, 1946
Hall of Fame Inductee – 1972

YEAR	TEAM	LG	POS	G	AB	R	H	2B	3B	HR	RBI	TB	AVG	SLG
1946	NY	AL	C	7	22	3	8	1	0	2	4	15	.364	.682
1947	NY	AL	C	83	293	41	82	15	3	11	54	136	.280	.464
1948	NY	AL	C	125	469	70	143	24	10	14	98	229	.305	.488
1949	NY	AL	C	116	415	59	115	20	2	20	91	199	.277	.480
1950	NY	AL	C	151	597	116	192	30	6	28	124	318	.322	.533
1951	NY	AL	C	141	547	92	161	19	4	27	88	269	.294	.492
1952	NY	AL	C	142	534	97	146	17	1	30	98	255	.273	.478
1953	NY	AL	C	137	503	80	149	23	5	27	108	263	.296	.523
1954	NY	AL	C	151	584	88	179	28	6	22	125	285	.307	.488
1955	NY	AL	C	147	541	84	147	20	3	27	108	254	.272	.470
1956	NY	AL	C	140	521	93	155	29	2	30	105	278	.298	.534
1957	NY	AL	C	134	482	74	121	14	2	24	82	211	.251	.438
1958	NY	AL	C	122	433	60	115	17	3	22	90	204	.266	.471
1959	NY	AL	C	131	472	64	134	25	1	19	69	218	.284	.462
1960	NY	AL	C	120	359	46	99	14	1	15	62	160	.276	.446
1961	NY	AL	OF	119	395	62	107	11	0	22	61	184	.271	.466
1962	NY	AL	C	86	232	25	52	8	0	10	35	90	.224	.388
1963	NY	AL	C	64	147	20	43	6	0	8	28	73	.293	.497
1965	NY	NL	C	4	9	1	2	0	0	0	0	2	.222	.222
TOTALS				**2120**	**7555**	**1175**	**2150**	**321**	**49**	**358**	**1430**	**3643**	**.285**	**.482**

Roger Philip "The Duke Of Tralee" Bresnahan
Bats: Right Throws: Right
Height: 5'9" Weight: 200 lbs.
Born: June 11, 1879 in Toledo, OH
Major League Debut: Aug. 27, 1897
Died: Dec. 4, 1944 in Toledo, OH
Hall of Fame Inductee – 1945

YEAR	TEAM	LG	POS	G	AB	R	H	2B	3B	HR	RBI	TB	AVG	SLG
1897	Was	NL	P	6	16	1	6	0	0	0	3	6	.375	.375
1900	Chi	NL	C	2	2	0	0	0	0	0	0	0	.000	.000
1901	Bal	AL	C	86	295	40	79	9	9	1	32	109	.268	.369
1902	Bal	AL	3B	65	235	30	64	8	6	4	34	96	.272	.409
1902	NY	NL	OF	51	178	16	51	9	3	1	22	69	.287	.388
1903	NY	NL	OF	113	406	87	142	30	8	4	55	200	.350	.493
1904	NY	NL	OF	109	402	81	114	22	7	5	33	165	.284	.410
1905	NY	NL	C	104	331	58	100	18	3	0	46	124	.302	.375
1906	NY	NL	C	124	405	69	114	22	4	0	43	144	.281	.356
1907	NY	NL	C	110	328	57	83	9	7	4	38	118	.253	.360
1908	NY	NL	C	140	449	70	127	25	3	1	54	161	.283	.359
1909	StL	NL	C	72	234	27	57	4	1	0	23	63	.244	.269
1910	StL	NL	C	88	234	35	65	15	3	0	27	86	.278	.368
1911	StL	NL	C	81	227	22	63	17	8	3	41	105	.278	.463
1912	StL	NL	C	48	108	8	36	7	2	1	15	50	.333	.463
1913	Chi	NL	C	69	162	20	37	5	2	1	21	49	.228	.302
1914	Chi	NL	C	101	248	42	69	10	4	0	24	87	.278	.351
1915	Chi	NL	C	77	221	19	45	8	1	1	19	58	.204	.262
TOTALS				**1446**	**4481**	**682**	**1252**	**218**	**71**	**26**	**530**	**1690**	**.279**	**.377**

Roy Campanella
Bats: Right Throws: Right
Height: 5'8" Weight: 200 lbs.
Born: Nov. 19, 1921 in Philadelphia, PA
Major League Debut: April 20, 1948
Died: June 26, 1993 in Woodland Hills, CA
Hall of Fame Inductee – 1969

YEAR	TEAM	LG	POS	G	AB	R	H	2B	3B	HR	RBI	TB	AVG	SLG
1948	Bro	NL	C	83	279	32	72	11	3	9	45	116	.258	.416
1949	Bro	NL	C	130	436	65	125	22	2	22	82	217	.287	.498
1950	Bro	NL	C	126	437	70	123	19	3	31	89	241	.281	.551
1951	Bro	NL	C	143	505	90	164	33	1	33	108	298	.325	.590
1952	Bro	NL	C	128	468	73	126	18	1	22	97	212	.269	.453
1953	Bro	NL	C	144	519	103	162	26	3	41	142	317	.312	.611
1954	Bro	NL	C	111	397	43	82	14	3	19	51	159	.207	.401
1955	Bro	NL	C	123	446	81	142	20	1	32	107	260	.318	.583
1956	Bro	NL	C	124	388	39	85	6	1	20	73	153	.219	.394
1957	Bro	NL	C	103	330	31	80	9	0	13	62	128	.242	.388
TOTALS				**1215**	**4205**	**627**	**1161**	**178**	**18**	**242**	**856**	**2101**	**.276**	**.500**

Gary Edmund Carter
Bats: Right Throws: Right
Height: 6'2" Weight: 215 lbs.
Born: April 8, 1954 in Culver City, CA
Major League Debut: Sept. 16, 1974
Hall of Fame Inductee – 2003

YEAR	TEAM	LG	POS	G	AB	R	H	2B	3B	HR	RBI	TB	AVG	SLG
1974	Mon	NL	C	9	27	5	11	0	1	1	6	16	.407	.593
1975	Mon	NL	OF	144	503	58	136	20	1	17	68	209	.270	.416
1976	Mon	AL	C	91	311	31	68	8	1	6	38	96	.219	.309
1977	Mon	AL	C	154	522	86	148	29	2	31	84	274	.284	.525
1978	Mon	NL	C	157	533	76	136	27	1	20	72	225	.255	.422
1979	Mon	NL	C	141	505	74	143	26	5	22	75	245	.283	.485
1980	Mon	NL	C	154	549	76	145	25	5	29	101	267	.264	.486
1981	Mon	NL	C	100	374	48	94	20	2	16	68	166	.251	.444
1982	Mon	NL	C	154	557	91	163	32	1	29	97	284	.293	.510
1983	Mon	NL	C	145	541	63	146	37	3	17	79	240	.270	.444
1984	Mon	NL	C	159	596	75	175	32	1	27	106	290	.294	.487
1985	NY	NL	C	149	555	83	156	17	1	32	100	271	.281	.488
1986	NY	NL	C	132	490	81	125	14	2	24	105	215	.255	.439
1987	NY	NL	C	139	523	55	123	18	2	20	83	205	.235	.392
1988	NY	NL	C	130	455	39	110	16	2	11	46	163	.242	.358
1989	NY	NL	C	50	153	14	28	8	0	2	15	42	.183	.275
1990	SF	NL	C	92	244	24	62	10	0	9	27	99	.254	.406
1991	LA	NL	C	101	248	22	61	14	0	6	26	93	.246	.375
1992	Mon	NL	C	95	285	24	62	18	1	5	29	97	.218	.340
TOTALS				**2296**	**7971**	**1025**	**2092**	**371**	**31**	**324**	**1225**	**3497**	**.262**	**.439**

Gordon Stanley Cochrane
Bats: Left Throws: Right
Height: 5'10" Weight: 180 lbs.
Born: April 6, 1903 in Bridgewater, MA
Major League Debut: April 14, 1925
Died: June 28, 1962 in Lake Forest, IL
Hall of Fame Inductee – 1947

YEAR	TEAM	LG	POS	G	AB	R	H	2B	3B	HR	RBI	TB	AVG	SLG
1925	Phi	AL	C	134	420	69	139	21	5	6	55	188	.331	.448
1926	Phi	AL	C	120	370	50	101	8	9	8	47	151	.273	.408
1927	Phi	AL	C	126	432	80	146	20	6	12	80	214	.338	.495
1928	Phi	AL	C	131	468	92	137	26	12	10	57	217	.293	.464
1929	Phi	AL	C	135	514	113	170	37	8	7	95	244	.331	.475
1930	Phi	AL	C	130	487	110	174	42	5	10	85	256	.357	.526
1931	Phi	AL	C	122	459	87	160	31	6	17	89	254	.349	.553
1932	Phi	AL	C	139	518	118	152	35	4	23	112	264	.293	.510
1933	Phi	AL	C	130	429	104	138	30	4	15	60	221	.322	.515
1934	Det	AL	C	129	437	74	140	32	1	2	76	180	.320	.412
1935	Det	AL	C	115	411	93	131	33	3	5	47	185	.319	.450
1936	Det	AL	C	44	126	24	34	8	0	2	17	48	.270	.381
1937	Det	AL	C	27	98	27	30	10	1	2	12	48	.306	.490
TOTALS				**1482**	**5169**	**1041**	**1652**	**333**	**64**	**119**	**832**	**2470**	**.320**	**.478**

William Malcolm Dickey
Bats: Left Throws: Right
Height: 6'1" Weight: 185 lbs.
Born: June 6, 1907 in Bastrop, LA
Major League Debut: Aug. 15, 1928
Died: Nov. 12, 1993 in Little Rock, AR
Hall of Fame Inductee – 1954

YEAR	TEAM	LG	POS	G	AB	R	H	2B	3B	HR	RBI	TB	AVG	SLG
1928	NY	AL	C	10	15	1	3	1	1	0	2	6	.200	.400
1929	NY	AL	OF	130	447	60	145	30	6	10	65	217	.324	.485
1930	NY	AL	C	109	366	55	124	25	7	5	65	178	.339	.486
1931	NY	AL	C	130	477	65	156	17	10	6	78	211	.327	.442
1932	NY	AL	C	108	423	66	131	20	4	15	84	204	.310	.482
1933	NY	AL	C	130	478	58	152	24	8	14	97	234	.318	.490
1934	NY	AL	C	104	395	56	127	24	4	12	72	195	.322	.494
1935	NY	AL	C	120	448	54	125	26	6	14	81	205	.279	.458
1936	NY	AL	C	112	423	99	153	26	8	22	107	261	.362	.617
1937	NY	AL	C	140	530	87	176	35	2	29	133	302	.332	.570
1938	NY	AL	C	132	454	84	142	27	4	27	115	258	.313	.568
1939	NY	AL	C	128	480	98	145	23	3	24	105	246	.302	.513
1940	NY	AL	C	106	372	45	92	11	1	9	54	132	.247	.355
1941	NY	AL	C	109	348	35	99	15	5	7	71	145	.284	.417
1942	NY	AL	C	82	268	28	79	13	1	2	37	100	.295	.373
1943	NY	AL	C	85	242	29	85	18	2	4	33	119	.351	.492
1946	NY	AL	C	54	134	10	35	8	0	2	10	49	.261	.366
TOTALS				**1789**	**6300**	**930**	**1969**	**343**	**72**	**202**	**1209**	**3062**	**.313**	**.486**

William "Buck" Ewing
Bats: Right Throws: Right
Height: 5'10" Weight: 188 lbs.
Born: Oct. 17, 1859 in Hoagland, OH
Major League Debut: Sept. 9, 1880
Died: Oct. 20, 1906 in Cincinnati, OH
Hall of Fame Inductee – 1936

YEAR	TEAM	LG	POS	G	AB	R	H	2B	3B	HR	RBI	TB	AVG	SLG
1880	Try	NL	C	13	45	1	8	1	0	0	5	9	.178	.200
1881	Try	NL	C	67	272	40	68	14	7	0	25	96	.250	.353
1882	Try	NL	3B	74	328	67	89	16	11	2	29	133	.271	.405
1883	NY	NL	C	88	376	90	114	11	13	10	41	181	.303	.481
1884	NY	NL	C	94	382	90	106	15	20	3	41	170	.277	.445
1885	NY	NL	C	81	342	81	104	15	12	6	63	161	.304	.471
1886	NY	NL	C	73	275	59	85	11	7	4	31	122	.309	.444
1887	NY	NL	3B	77	318	83	97	17	13	6	44	158	.305	.497
1888	NY	NL	C	103	415	83	127	18	15	6	58	193	.306	.465
1889	NY	NL	C	99	407	91	133	23	13	4	87	194	.327	.477
1890	NY	PL	C	83	352	98	119	19	15	8	72	192	.338	.545
1891	NY	NL	2B	14	49	8	17	2	1	0	18	21	.347	.429
1892	NY	NL	1B	105	393	58	122	10	15	8	76	186	.310	.473
1893	Cle	NL	OF	116	500	117	172	28	15	6	122	248	.344	.496
1894	Cle	NL	OF	53	211	32	53	12	4	2	39	79	.251	.374
1895	Cin	NL	1B	105	434	90	138	24	13	5	94	203	.318	.468
1896	Cin	NL	1B	69	263	41	73	14	4	1	38	98	.278	.373
1897	Cin	NL	1B	1	1	0	0	0	0	0	0	0	.000	.000
TOTALS				**1315**	**5363**	**1129**	**1625**	**250**	**178**	**71**	**883**	**2444**	**.303**	**.456**

Richard Benjamin Ferrell

Bats: Right Throws: Right

Height: 5'10" Weight: 160 lbs.

Born: Oct. 12, 1905 in Durham, NC

Major League Debut: April 19, 1929

Died: July 27, 1995 in Bloomfield Hills, MI

Hall of Fame Inductee – 1984

YEAR	TEAM	LG	POS	G	AB	R	H	2B	3B	HR	RBI	TB	AVG	SLG
1929	StL	AL	C	64	144	21	33	6	1	0	20	41	.229	.285
1930	StL	AL	C	101	314	43	84	18	4	1	41	113	.268	.360
1931	StL	AL	C	117	386	47	118	30	4	3	57	165	.306	.427
1932	StL	AL	C	126	438	67	138	30	5	2	65	184	.315	.420
1933	StL	AL	C	22	72	8	18	2	0	1	5	23	.250	.319
1933	Bos	AL	C	118	421	50	125	19	4	3	72	161	.297	.382
1934	Bos	AL	C	132	437	50	130	29	4	1	48	170	.297	.389
1935	Bos	AL	C	133	458	54	138	34	4	3	61	189	.301	.413
1936	Bos	AL	C	121	410	59	128	27	5	8	55	189	.312	.461
1937	Bos	AL	C	18	65	8	20	2	0	1	4	25	.308	.385
1937	Was	AL	C	86	279	31	64	6	0	1	32	73	.229	.262
1938	Was	AL	C	135	411	55	120	24	5	1	58	157	.292	.382
1939	Was	AL	C	87	274	32	77	13	1	0	31	92	.281	.336
1940	Was	AL	C	103	326	35	89	18	2	0	28	111	.273	.340
1941	Was	AL	C	21	66	8	18	5	0	0	13	23	.273	.348
1941	StL	AL	C	100	321	30	81	14	3	2	23	107	.252	.333
1942	StL	AL	C	99	273	20	61	6	1	0	26	69	.223	.253
1943	StL	AL	C	74	209	12	50	7	0	0	20	57	.239	.273
1944	Was	AL	C	99	339	14	94	11	1	0	25	107	.277	.316
1945	Was	AL	C	91	286	33	76	12	1	1	38	93	.266	.325
1947	Was	AL	C	37	99	10	30	11	0	0	12	41	.303	.414
TOTALS				**1884**	**6028**	**687**	**1692**	**324**	**45**	**28**	**734**	**2190**	**.281**	**.363**

Carlton Ernest "Pudge" Fisk
Bats: Right Throws: Right
Height: 6'2" Weight: 220 lbs.
Born: Dec. 26, 1947 in Bellows Falls, VT
Major League Debut: Sept. 18, 1969
Hall of Fame Inductee – 2000

YEAR	TEAM	LG	POS	G	AB	R	H	2B	3B	HR	RBI	TB	AVG	SLG
1969	Bos	AL	C	2	5	0	0	0	0	0	0	0	.000	.000
1971	Bos	AL	C	14	48	7	15	2	1	2	6	25	.313	.521
1972	Bos	AL	C	131	457	74	134	28	9	22	61	246	.293	.538
1973	Bos	AL	C	135	508	65	125	21	0	26	71	224	.246	.441
1974	Bos	AL	C	52	187	36	56	12	1	11	26	103	.299	.551
1975	Bos	AL	C	79	263	47	87	14	4	10	52	139	.331	.529
1976	Bos	AL	C	134	487	76	124	17	5	17	58	202	.255	.415
1977	Bos	AL	C	152	536	106	169	26	3	26	102	279	.315	.521
1978	Bos	AL	C	157	571	94	162	39	5	20	88	271	.284	.475
1979	Bos	AL	DH	91	320	49	87	23	2	10	42	144	.272	.450
1980	Bos	AL	C	131	478	73	138	25	3	18	62	223	.289	.467
1981	Chi	AL	C	96	338	44	89	12	0	7	45	122	.263	.361
1982	Chi	AL	C	135	476	66	127	17	3	14	65	192	.267	.403
1983	Chi	AL	C	138	488	85	141	26	4	26	86	253	.289	.518
1984	Chi	AL	C	102	359	54	83	20	1	21	43	168	.231	.468
1985	Chi	AL	C	153	543	85	129	23	1	37	107	265	.238	.488
1986	Chi	AL	C	125	457	42	101	11	0	14	63	154	.221	.337
1987	Chi	AL	C	135	454	68	116	22	1	23	71	209	.256	.460
1988	Chi	AL	C	76	253	37	70	8	1	19	50	137	.277	.542
1989	Chi	AL	C	103	375	47	110	25	2	13	68	178	.293	.475
1990	Chi	AL	C	137	452	65	129	21	0	18	65	204	.285	.451
1991	Chi	AL	C	134	460	42	111	25	0	18	74	190	.241	.413
1992	Chi	AL	C	62	188	12	43	4	1	3	21	58	.229	.309
1993	Chi	AL	C	25	53	2	10	0	0	1	4	13	.189	.245
TOTALS				**2499**	**8756**	**1276**	**2356**	**421**	**47**	**376**	**1330**	**3999**	**.269**	**.457**

Joshua Gibson
Bats: Right Throws: Right
Height: 6'1" Weight: 215 lbs.
Born: Dec. 21, 1911 in Buene Vista, CA
Major League Debut: June 19, 1930
Died: Jan. 20, 1947 in Pittsburgh, PA
Hall of Fame Inductee - 1972

(No statistics kept)

Charles Leo "Gabby" Hartnett

Bats: Right Throws: Right

Height: 6'1" Weight: 195 lbs.

Born: Dec. 20, 1900 in Woonsocket, RI

Major League Debut: April 12, 1922

Died: Dec. 20, 1972 in Park Ridge, IL

Hall of Fame Inductee – 1955

YEAR	TEAM	LG	POS	G	AB	R	H	2B	3B	HR	RBI	TB	AVG	SLG
1922	Chi	NL	C	31	72	4	14	1	1	0	4	17	.194	.236
1923	Chi	NL	C	85	231	28	62	12	2	8	39	102	.268	.442
1924	Chi	NL	C	111	354	56	106	17	7	16	67	185	.299	.523
1925	Chi	NL	C	117	398	61	115	28	3	24	67	221	.289	.555
1926	Chi	NL	C	93	284	35	78	25	3	8	41	133	.275	.468
1927	Chi	NL	C	127	449	56	132	32	5	10	80	204	.294	.454
1928	Chi	NL	C	120	388	61	117	26	9	14	57	203	.302	.523
1929	Chi	NL	C	25	22	2	6	2	1	1	9	13	.273	.591
1930	Chi	NL	C	141	508	84	172	31	3	37	122	320	.339	.630
1931	Chi	NL	C	116	380	53	107	32	1	8	70	165	.282	.434
1932	Chi	NL	C	121	406	52	110	25	3	12	52	177	.271	.436
1933	Chi	NL	C	140	490	55	135	21	4	16	88	212	.276	.433
1934	Chi	NL	C	130	438	58	131	21	1	22	90	220	.299	.502
1935	Chi	NL	C	116	413	67	142	32	6	13	91	225	.344	.545
1936	Chi	NL	C	121	424	49	130	25	6	7	64	188	.307	.443
1937	Chi	NL	C	110	356	47	126	21	6	12	82	195	.354	.548
1938	Chi	NL	C	88	299	40	82	19	1	10	59	133	.274	.445
1939	Chi	NL	C	97	306	36	85	18	2	12	59	143	.278	.467
1940	Chi	NL	C	37	64	3	17	3	0	1	12	23	.266	.359
1941	NY	NL	C	64	150	20	45	5	0	5	26	65	.300	.433
TOTALS				**1990**	**6432**	**867**	**1912**	**396**	**64**	**236**	**1179**	**3144**	**.297**	**.489**

Ernesto Natali "Schnozz" or "Bocci" Lombardi

Bats: Right Throws: Right
Height: 6'3" Weight: 230 lbs.
Born: April 6, 1908 in Oakland, CA
Major League Debut: April 15, 1931
Died: Sept. 26, 1977 in Santa Cruz, CA
Hall of Fame Inductee – 1986

YEAR	TEAM	LG	POS	G	AB	R	H	2B	3B	HR	RBI	TB	AVG	SLG
1931	Bro	NL	C	73	182	20	54	7	1	4	23	75	.297	.412
1932	Cin	NL	C	118	413	43	125	22	9	11	68	198	.303	.479
1933	Cin	NL	C	107	350	30	99	21	1	4	47	134	.283	.383
1934	Cin	NL	C	132	417	42	127	19	4	9	62	181	.305	.434
1935	Cin	NL	C	120	332	36	114	23	3	12	64	179	.343	.539
1936	Cin	NL	C	121	387	42	129	23	2	12	68	192	.333	.496
1937	Cin	NL	C	120	368	41	123	22	1	9	59	174	.334	.473
1938	Cin	NL	C	129	489	60	167	30	1	19	95	256	.342	.524
1939	Cin	NL	C	130	450	43	129	26	2	20	85	219	.287	.487
1940	Cin	NL	C	109	376	50	120	22	0	14	74	184	.319	.489
1941	Cin	NL	C	117	398	33	105	12	1	10	60	149	.264	.374
1942	Bos	NL	C	105	309	32	102	14	0	11	46	149	.330	.482
1943	NY	NL	C	104	295	19	90	7	0	10	51	127	.305	.431
1944	NY	NL	C	117	373	37	95	13	0	10	58	138	.255	.370
1945	NY	NL	C	115	368	46	113	7	1	19	70	179	.307	.486
1946	NY	NL	C	88	238	19	69	4	1	12	39	111	.290	.466
1947	NY	NL	C	48	110	8	31	5	0	4	21	48	.282	.436
TOTALS				**1853**	**5855**	**601**	**1792**	**277**	**27**	**190**	**990**	**2693**	**.306**	**.460**

Raymond William "Cracker" Schalk
Bats: Right Throws: Right
Height: 5'9" Weight: 165 lbs.
Born: Aug. 12, 1892 in Harvel, IL
Major League Debut: Aug. 11, 1912
Died: May 19, 1970 in Chicago, IL
Hall of Fame Inductee – 1955

YEAR	TEAM	LG	POS	G	AB	R	H	2B	3B	HR	RBI	TB	AVG	SLG
1912	Chi	AL	C	23	63	7	18	2	0	0	8	20	.286	.317
1913	Chi	AL	C	129	401	38	98	15	5	1	38	126	.244	.314
1914	Chi	AL	C	136	392	30	106	13	2	0	36	123	.270	.314
1915	Chi	AL	C	135	413	46	110	14	4	1	54	135	.266	.327
1916	Chi	AL	C	129	410	36	95	12	9	0	41	125	.232	.305
1917	Chi	AL	C	140	424	48	96	12	5	2	51	124	.226	.292
1918	Chi	AL	C	108	333	35	73	6	3	0	22	85	.219	.255
1919	Chi	AL	C	131	394	57	111	9	3	0	34	126	.282	.320
1920	Chi	AL	C	151	485	64	131	25	5	1	61	169	.270	.348
1921	Chi	AL	C	128	416	32	105	24	4	0	47	137	.252	.329
1922	Chi	AL	C	142	442	57	124	22	3	4	60	164	.281	.371
1923	Chi	AL	C	123	382	42	87	12	2	1	44	106	.228	.277
1924	Chi	AL	C	57	153	15	30	4	2	1	11	41	.196	.268
1925	Chi	AL	C	125	343	44	94	18	1	0	52	114	.274	.332
1926	Chi	AL	C	82	226	26	60	9	1	0	32	71	.265	.314
1927	Chi	AL	C	16	26	2	6	2	0	0	2	8	.231	.308
1928	Chi	AL	C	2	1	0	1	0	0	0	1	1	1.000	1.000
1929	NY	NL	C	5	2	0	0	0	0	0	0	0	.000	.000
TOTALS				**1762**	**5306**	**579**	**1345**	**199**	**49**	**11**	**594**	**1674**	**.253**	**.316**

Gold Glove Winners—Catchers

The Gold Glove Award was first presented by Rawlings in 1957 to honor the nine best fielders in each league at their respective positions. The award is determined by a vote of managers and coaches from each major league team who are not eligible to vote for their own players.

National League	American League
1957	
One Winner Only	Sherm Lollar (Chicago)
1958	
Del Crandall (Milwaukee)	Sherm Lollar (Chicago)
1959	
Del Crandall (Milwaukee)	Sherm Lollar (Chicago)
1960	
Del Crandall (Milwaukee)	Earl Battey (Washington)
1961	
Johnny Roseboro (Los Angeles)	Earl Battey (Chicago)
1962	
Del Crandall (Milwaukee)	Earl Battey (Minnesota)
1963	
Johnny Edwards (Cincinnati)	Elston Howard (New York)
1964	
Johnny Edwards (Cincinnati)	Elston Howard (New York)
1965	
Joe Torre (Milwaukee)	Bill Freehan (Detroit)
1966	
Johnny Roseboro (Los Angeles)	Bill Freehan (Detroit)
1967	
Randy Hundley (Chicago)	Bill Freehan (Detroit)
1968	
Johnny Bench (Cincinnati)	Bill Freehan (Detroit)

1969	
Johnny Bench (Cincinnati)	Bill Freehan (Detroit)
1970	
Johnny Bench (Cincinnati)	Ray Fosse (Cleveland)
1971	
Johnny Bench (Cincinnati)	Ray Fosse (Cleveland)
1972	
Johnny Bench (Cincinnati)	Carlton Fisk (Boston)
1973	
Johnny Bench (Cincinnati)	Thurman Munson (New York)
1974	
Johnny Bench (Cincinnati)	Thurman Munson (New York)
1975	
Johnny Bench (Cincinnati)	Thurman Munson (New York)
1976	
Johnny Bench (Cincinnati)	Jim Sundberg (Texas)
1977	
Johnny Bench (Cincinnati)	Jim Sundberg (Texas)
1978	
Bob Boone (Philadelphia)	Jim Sundberg (Texas)
1979	
Bob Boone (Philadelphia)	Jim Sundberg (Texas)
1980	
Gary Carter (Montreal)	Jim Sundberg (Texas)
1981	
Gary Carter (Montreal)	Jim Sundberg (Texas)
1982	
Gary Carter (Montreal)	Bob Boone (California)
1983	
Tony Pena (Pittsburgh)	Lance Parrish (Detroit)

1984	
Tony Pena (Pittsburgh)	Lance Parrish (Detroit)
1985	
Tony Pena (Pittsburgh)	Lance Parrish (Detroit)
1986	
Jody Davis (Chicago)	Bob Boone (California)
1987	
Mike LaValliere (Pittsburgh)	Bob Boone (California)
1988	
Benito Santiago (San Diego)	Bob Boone ((California)
1989	
Benito Santiago (San Diego)	Bob Boone ((Kansas City)
1990	
Benito Santiago (San Diego)	Sandy Alomar, Jr. (Cleveland)
1991	
Tom Pagnozzi (St. Louis)	Tony Pena ((Boston)
1992	
Tom Pagnozzi (St. Louis)	Ivan Rodriguez (Texas)
1993	
Kirt Manwaring (San Francisco)	Ivan Rodriguez (Texas)
1994	
Tom Pagnozzi (St. Louis)	Ivan Rodriguez (Texas)
1995	
Charles Johnson ((Florida)	Ivan Rodriguez (Texas)
1996	
Charles Johnson (Florida)	Ivan Rodriguez (Texas)
1997	
Charles Johnson (Florida)	Ivan Rodriguez (Texas)
1998	
Charles Johnson (Los Angeles)	Ivan Rodriguez ((Texas)

1999	
Mike Lieberthal (Philadelphia)	Ivan Rodriguez (Texas)
2000	
Mike Matheny (St. Louis)	Ivan Rodriguez (Texas)
2001	
Brad Ausmus (Houston)	Ivan Rodriguez (Texas)
2002	
Brad Ausmus (Houston)	Bengie Molina (Anaheim)
2003	
Mike Matheny (St. Louis)	Bengie Molina (Anaheim)
2004	
Mike Matheny (St. Louis)	Ivan Rodriguez (Detroit)

Most Valuable Players—Catchers

NAME	TEAM	LEAGUE	YEAR
Bob O'Farrell	St. Louis Cardinals	National	1926
Mickey Cochrane	Detroit Tigers	American	1928, '34
Gabby Hartnett	Chicago Cubs	National	1935
Ernie Lombardi	Cincinnati Reds	National	1938
Yogi Berra	New York Yankees	American	1951, '54, '55
Roy Campanella	Brooklyn Dodgers	National	1951, '53, '55
Elston Howard	New York Yankees	American	1963
Johnny Bench	Cincinnati Reds	National	1970, 72
Thurman Munson	New York Yankees	American	1976

Rookies of the Year—Catchers

NAME	TEAM	LEAGUE	YEAR
Johnny Bench	Cincinnati Reds	National	1968
Thurman Munson	New York Yankees	American	1970
Earl Williams	Atlanta Braves	National	1971
Carlton Fisk	Boston Red Sox	American	1972
Benito Santiago	San Diego Padres	National	1987
Sandy Alomar, Jr.	Cleveland Indians	American	1990
Mike Piazza	Los Angeles Dodgers	National	1993

Retired Numbers—Catchers

NAME	TEAM	NUMBER
Johnny Bench	Cincinnati Reds	5
*Yogi Berra	New York Yankees	8
Roy Campanella	Los Angeles Dodgers	39
Gary Carter	Montreal Expos	8
*Bill Dickey	New York Yankees	8
Carlton Fisk	Chicago White Sox	72
Elston Howard	New York Yankees	32
Thurman Munson	New York Yankees	15

* In 1972 the Yankees retired number 8 in honor of both Berra and Dickey

Great Catchers of the Negro Leagues Who Are Not in the Hall of Fame

Larry Brown	1919-1948
Frank Duncan	1921-1948
"Buck" Ewing	1920-1941
Raleigh "Biz" Mackey	1922-1947
Bruce Petway	1906-1925
Ted "Double Duty" Radcliffe	1928-1950
Louis Santop	1909-1926
Quincy Trouppe	1930-1952

One-Game Catchers since 1940 (entire Major League career lasted one game)

NAME	TEAM	YEAR
Jim Devlin	Cleveland Indians	1944
Frank Estrada	New York Mets	1971
Jack Feller	Detroit Tigers	1958
Dick Hahn	Washington Senators	1940
Buddy Hancken	Philadelphia Athletics	1940
John Levovich	Philadelphia Athletics	1941
John Lickert	Boston Red Sox	1981
Dave Liddell	New York Mets	1990
Chuck Lindstrom	Chicago White Sox	1958
Steve Lomasney	Boston Red Sox	1999
Eric Mackenzie	Kansas City Athletics	1955
Charlie Marshall	St. Louis Cardinals	1941
Tom Patton	Baltimore Orioles	1957

Bill Peterman	Philadelphia Phillies	1942
George Pfister	Brooklyn Dodgers	1941
Bob Scherbarth	Boston Red Sox	1950
Nick Testa	San Francisco Giants	1958
Milt Welch	Detroit Tigers	1945
Tom Yerwcic	Detroit Tigers	1957
Bart Zeller	St. Louis Cardinals	1970

Nine Catchers You've Probably Never Heard Of

The following catchers aren't famous, but they're stories are definitely worth recalling. Their lives involved a good bit of drama, in some cases humorous and in others tragic, and what makes the stories memorable does not always involve the game of baseball.

1. Marty Bergen: Martin "Marty" Bergen was born in North Brookfield, Massachusetts, on October 25, 1871. He made his major league debut as a member of the local Boston Beaneaters (previously known as the Red Caps, and later known as the Boston Doves, Bees, Braves, Milwaukee Braves and Atlanta Braves) on April 25, 1896. Bergen was the starting catcher all four years he played with the Beaneaters, and the team won back-to-back National League pennants in 1897 and 1898 behind the pitching of Bergen's batterymate and future Hall of Famer Kid Nichols. Bergen maintained a career batting average of .265.

On October 14, 1898, the *Washington Post* noted that

Bergen "of nerves of steel and a throwing arm as true as a bullet from the gun of Ira Paine, is indeed the premier of the backstops of the major league. Bergen's work as a chance-taker eclipses the old-fashioned safety play of those backstops who lack the nerve to whisk the ball around the infield at critical points in a game."

The July 25, 1899, *Post* profiles a different catcher: "Backstop Marty Bergen, of the champions, has recovered from his annual attack of sulks. Though Bergen has the talents of a Ewing or a Robinson as a backstop, he is sullen, suspicious, and all the diplomacy and powers that [Boston manager Frank] Selee can muster to pluck the thorns from Marty's ungovernable temper."

Two days later the *Post* continued to paint Bergen as an ill-tempered troublemaker, calling him "about as tractable and lamblike as a Texas steer." The column goes on to relate that Bergen once went AWOL while playing for Kansas City of the Western League, and failed to report for a week. "Bergen," the article continues, "will probably be sold or exchanged at the first opportune moment."

Later that season, Bergen suffered a broken hip, an injury presumed to be career-threatening, and on January 19, 1900, killed his wife and two children with an axe on the family farm in North Brookfield before slitting his own throat with a straight razor. Of all Bergen's baseball teammates and opponents, only Connie Mack and Boston center fielder Billy Hamilton attended the funeral.

2. Bill Bergen: Bill Bergen was also born in North Brookfield, Massachusetts, and made his major league debut with the Cincinnati Reds just sixteen months after his brother's suicide. He developed into one of the best-throwing catchers and worst-hitting players—at any position—of the early twentieth century. In fact, Bill Bergen is the worst "everyday" hitter in major league history, with a career batting average of just .170, forty-two points lower than any other player with 2500 or more at-bats.

The April 7, 1910 *Washington Post* relates that "Bill isn't much with the wood; in fact, the occasion when he has slammed out hits are so rare that he can recall the dates when they were made."

Besides reigning as baseball's career worst hitter, Bergen also set a single-season low of .139 in 1909. But that same year he racked up 202 assists, the ninth-best total ever for a catcher. His throwing success is even more remarkable when one takes into consideration his flat-footed throwing motion.

The *Washington Post* of July 7, 1906, states that "Gotham scribes are calling Bill Bergen (now playing for the Brooklyn Superbas) the greatest catcher in the big league as far as stealing bases go. Bill is said to be one of the few backstops to throw perfectly without taking a forward step."

Bergen set a twentieth century record (now tied) on August 23, 1909, by throwing out six baserunners in a nine-inning game against the St. Louis Cardinals.

3. Nick Testa: Nick Testa, the son of Italian immigrants, grew up in the Bronx and was a catcher at Christopher Columbus High School. While playing high school ball, Testa was offered a football scholarship at the University of Florida after a play at the plate left the opposition runner unconscious.

Testa signed with the New York Giants in 1947 for a five-hundred-dollar bonus and was assigned to Class D ball. With the exception of two years in the service during the Korean War, Testa played in the Giants minor league system for the next ten years. After backup catcher Bill Sarni suffered a career-ending heart attack during the Giants 1957 spring training, Testa was invited to big league camp in 1958. That was the year the Giants moved to San Francisco, and Testa made the club as a third-string catcher. The Bronx native made himself useful by warming up pitchers in the bullpen and throwing extra batting practice to Giants regulars.

On April 23, 1958, the Giants hosted the St. Louis Cardinals at Seals Stadium and the Cardinals held a 6-2 lead going into the bottom of the eighth. The Giants managed two runs in their half of the inning, and Testa was brought in as a pinch-runner, his first major league appearance. He donned the gear to catch Marv Grissom in the top of the ninth and committed an error chasing a wind-blown pop foul. The Cardinals added a run on a Stan Musial double so the Giants trailed 7-4 going into their last at-bat.

In the bottom of the ninth San Francisco managed to load the bases, bringing Testa into the on-deck circle, but

Giants shortstop Daryl Spencer hit a grand slam home run over the left field fence to win the game and cost Nick Testa his only chance at a major league at-bat.

4. Doug Gwosdz: Nicknames have certainly taken a turn towards the unimaginative in the past fifty years. The New York Yankees, in the past few seasons, probably rank as the most inventive team on the basis of Roger "Rocket" Clemens and David "Boomer" Wells alone. Unfortunately, two non-name-based monikers count as creative nowadays (it should be noted that both Clemens and Wells joined, and have since departed, the Yanks with their nicknames already attached). So perhaps the most inventive catcher nickname of the past forty years is Doug "Eyechart" Gwosdz, based of course on his hard-to-spell surname.

Though a second round pick by the Padres in 1978, Gwosdz had little success as a professional. He played four seasons in the majors, all with the Pads, backing up Terry Kennedy (or backing up Kennedy's backup). In those four years he played a total of sixty-nine games and came to the plate 104 times. Gwosdz managed eight RBI and a career batting average of .144. His lone home run came at Jack Murphy Stadium in the second game of a doubleheader on August 21, 1983, against Montreal's Bill Gullickson with two men on.

5. Sid Gautreaux: Speaking of nicknames, most baseball fans are familiar with Hall of Famer Carlton "Pudge" Fisk and likely Hall of Famer Ivan "Pudge" Rodriguez, but did anyone know there was a third major league catcher named Pudge?

Sid "Pudge" Gautreaux played for the Casey Stengel-managed 1936 Brooklyn Dodgers and the 1937 Brooklyn Dodgers managed by Burleigh Grimes. Stengel's club finished seventh out of eight National League teams, and the coaching change yielded a sixth-place finish.

Gautreaux's stat line is a rarity in that he played in eighty-six games as a major leaguer but had only eighty-one at-bats. Primarily used as a pinch-hitter, Gautreaux only played fifteen games in the field, all at catcher, in 1936 behind Dodgers starter (and future pitching coach) Ray Berres. In Gautreaux's final season he came to the plate eleven times, walked once and hit a two-run double for the final safety of his career. He committed one error behind the plate and compiled sixteen RBI despite never garnering anything longer than a two-base hit.

Following his term with the Dodgers, Gautreaux played minor league ball, including a stint with the Memphis Chicks, where once again his primary role was that of pinch-hitter. Gautreaux played for the Army baseball team during World War II and died in 1980 in Morgan City, Louisiana, thirty miles from where he was born.

6. Clint Courtney: Clint Courtney was a left-handed-batting catcher, a valuable commodity when managers saw the position as a natural platoon. Courtney played eleven major league seasons, all in the American League. He was selected as *The Sporting News* American League Rookie of the Year in 1952 (he finished second in the Baseball

Writers voting to A's pitcher Harry Byrd).

Despite the stereotype that came with being the first major league catcher to wear eyeglasses behind the plate, Clint Courtney was a tough competitor—a very tough competitor. Nicknamed "Scrap Iron," Courtney was fined a hundred dollars and suspended three days as a rookie for spiking Billy Martin and then punching him when Martin tried to retaliate. While playing for the Browns in 1953, Courtney collided with Yankees shortstop Phil Rizzuto at second base. Billy Martin, perhaps holding a grudge from the previous season, jumped onto Courtney's back, setting off a bench-clearing brawl that resulted in a then-American League record of $850 in fines.

In 1954, the Orioles first season in Baltimore after moving from St. Louis, Courtney smacked the first home run ever in Memorial Stadium off of White Sox pitcher Virgil Trucks. That same year Courtney struck out a league low seven times in 397 at-bats. He also finished in the league's top four in being hit by pitches in four separate seasons.

On top of being the first catcher to wear glasses, Courtney achieved another first in 1960. Back with Baltimore after five seasons with the Senators, Courtney was the first catcher to use the oversized mitt to cut down on passed balls attempting to catch knuckleballer Hoyt Wilhelm.

Courtney died of a heart attack in Rochester, New York in 1975 while manager of the Richmond Braves. He was forty-eight years old. Each year Richmond honors his memory by presenting the Clint Courtney Memorial Award to the team's most competitive player.

7. Willard Hershberger: Willard Hershberger began his professional career in the Yankees farm system when Bill Dickey, New York's future Hall of Fame catcher, was firmly entrenched as the starter. Since Dickey was a left-handed batter, Hershberger competed with fellow right-handed batter Buddy Rosar for the backup position. The Yankees chose Rosar, and Hershberger was sold to the Reds where he played behind another future Hall of Famer, Ernie Lombardi.

Hershberger was brought up to the big leagues in 1938, the year Lombardi was named National League MVP, and caught in thirty-nine games. In 1939 Hershberger took the number five (he wore number fifty the previous season) that would later be worn by another Hall of Fame Cincinnati catcher. Good with the bat, Hershberger appeared in sixty-three games that year and batted .345 with 32 RBI in 174 plate appearances. He played in his first World Series as well, getting into three games and managing a hit and a RBI in two at-bats as the Reds were swept in four games by the Yankees.

Injuries began to catch up with Lombardi in 1940, and for a time Hershberger, nicknamed "Herky-Jerky," "The Jitterbug" and "Hershie," was playing almost regularly. But on August 3, 1940, with his teammates at the ballpark, Willard Hershberger slit his throat with a straight razor in a Boston hotel room, becoming baseball's first in-season suicide.

According to the story, Hershberger blamed himself for a 5-4 loss to the New York Giants four days earlier. The Reds had a 4-1 lead with two out in bottom of the ninth inning when pitcher Bucky Walters gave up a walk, a home run, a second walk and a second home run to New York's Harry Danning. Hershberger even told several teammates and Reds manager Bill McKechnie that he had called the wrong pitches.

On the morning of August 3 Hershberger failed to show up at the park for the day's doubleheader, and McKechnie instructed a Reds official to call Hershberger at the hotel. Hershberger answered the phone, said he was sick, but that he would come to the ballpark. When he had not arrived by the seventh inning of the first game McKechnie sent Dan Cohen, a Cincinnati shoe store owner who had gone on the roadtrip, to the team's hotel. Cohen was admitted to the locked hotel room by a maid, and together they found Hershberger's body draped over the bathtub.

A newspaper report later described Hershberger as "given to fits of depression." Hershberger's father died of a self-inflicted gunshot wound in 1928, and Hershberger was the one who found the body.

The Reds managed to win a second straight National League pennant that season and faced the Tigers in the World Series. With Ernie Lombardi hampered by an ankle injury, forty-year-old Jimmie Wilson, who had been coaxed out of retirement by McKechnie to serve as Lombardi's backup, played most of the Series. Wilson batted .353 in six games as Cincinnati beat the Tigers four games to three. Willard Hershberger's mother was voted a full share of $5,803.

Thirteen years later, Ernie Lombardi, who retired from

baseball following the 1947 season, slit his own throat while visiting his sister in California. Lombardi's wife found him sprawled on the bed and immediately rushed him to the hospital where he eventually recovered.

8. Mike "Doc" Powers – A February 16, 1908 article in the Washington Post entitled "American League Has Many Wealthy Players on Its Teams" begins, "While there are no John D.'s among the ranks of baseball players, there are a number of famous diamond artists who could quit the game right now and give the traditional wolf the merry ha, ha, should he prowl around the front perzazzer."

Unfortunately no translation is available to let us know exactly what that sentence means, but later the article mentions that "Doc Powers of the Athletics is also in the rich men's class."Soon enough he would be making the news for a less pleasant reason than financial success.

Michael Riley "Doc" Powers, a real-life physician, attended the University of Notre Dame and was its first alumnus to reach the major leagues when he joined the National League's Louisville Colonels in 1898. He played a total of eleven seasons with the Colonels, the Washington Senators, the Philadelphia Athletics and the New York Highlanders, and appeared in one World Series—a losing effort in 1905 when John McGraw's New York Giants beat Connie Mack's Philadelphia Athletics four games to one.

Though Powers batted .251 and played in 116 games in 1901, the last several seasons of his career were spent as a backup to A's catcher Ossee Schrenkengost. Powers, who last batted over .200 in 1903, maintained his value to the Philadelphia club by serving as Eddie Plank's personal catcher.

On April 15, 1909 the A's hosted the first game at Philadelphia's Shibe Park. Plank was on the mound and Powers behind the plate in an 8-1 victory over the Boston Red Sox. After the contest Powers complained of intestinal pains attributed to running into a concrete wall during the game. Though operated on the following day, Powers passed away on April 26, the first major leaguer to die from injuries sustained on the playing field.

9. Harry Chiti: Harry Chiti was just seventeen years old when he made his major league debut with the Chicago Cubs on September 27, 1950. He shuttled back and forth between Chicago and the minors for three seasons before joining the military. Chiti came back to the Cubs in 1955 and was the starting catcher, just one of two seasons in which Chiti was a primary receiver.

In 1956, after batting .212 for the Cubs, he was traded to the Yankees, and he spent the 1957 season in their minor league system. The Kansas City Athletics acquired Chiti in the Rule 5 draft, and he rebounded with a .268 batting average in 103 games in 1958. It was with the Athletics staff—at times carrying as many as four knuckle-ball pitchers—that Chiti developed a reputation for being a strong knuckleball receiver.

After partial seasons with Kansas City and Detroit through 1961, he was traded to the Orioles, who traded him less than a month later to the Indians, who gave up Chiti up to the expansion Mets in late April of 1962.

Despite spending ten seasons in the major leagues, Chiti's notoriety is anchored in his fifteen games with New York. After batting less than .200 in his forty-one at-bats, the Mets sent Chiti back to Cleveland on June 15, 1962 as the player to be named later, which made Harry Chiti, in effect, the first player in major league history to be traded for himself.

Ever consider the Zodiac?

If you're wondering if you were born to be a catcher, you might want to check the zodiac. The thirty major league starting catchers on Opening Day 2003 possessed the following birth signs—six Aries, four Virgo, three Taurus, three Cancer, three Capricorn, three Pisces, three Libra, two Leo, and one each of Aquarius, Gemini and Sagittarius. No catching Scorpios were in the starting lineup on that day .

Which is not to say that Scorpios can't catch. Of the twenty-eight starting catchers on Opening Day in 1993, five were Leos, four Gemini, four Sagittarius, three Pisces, three Scorpios, two Taurus, two Virgo, two Libra and one each of Aries, Cancer, and Capricorn. No catching Aquarians were in the starting lineup on Opening Day 2003; otherwise, the list is almost an inverse from 2003.

Let's consider another list of backstops. Fourteen catchers have been elected to the Baseball Hall of Fame. The birth sign breakdown is as follows: three Sagittarius, three Aries, two Gemini, two Libra, and one each for Taurus, Leo,

Scorpio, and Capricorn. Here we're missing Cancer, Virgo, Pisces, and the beginning-to-look-like-non-catcher-appropriate Aquarians.

Of all starting catchers in 1993, 2003, and the fourteen Hall of Fame catchers, only one was born under the sign of Aquarius—Ken Huckaby, who after catching the opener would only play four more games in 2003. After a brief stop in Baltimore early in 2004, he finished the season with Texas. Clearly the stars are not aligned in his favor.

Likely Hall of Famer Ivan Rodriguez would be the fourth Sagittarian catcher in the Hall. If Mike Piazza joined the Hall of Fame he would be the first Virgo elected at the catcher position.

ABOUT THE AUTHOR

John Marvosa

The author with Elrod Hendricks

Rob Trucks is on the thin side of handsome, a veritable pole vault stanchion of a man. He is the author of *Cup of Coffee: The Very Short Careers of Eighteen Major League Pitchers* (Smallmouth Press, 2003) and *The Pleasure of Influence: Conversations with American Male Fiction Writers* (Purdue University Press, 2002). He lives and writes about baseball, literature and music for *Spin*, Newsweek.com, *BookForum, East Bay Express, Philadelphia Weekly, San Diego CityBeat, Cleveland Scene, Baltimore City Paper, Boulder Weekly,* and *Houston Press*, among other publications, from his closet-sized apartment in Long Island City, NY, but longs to move to Albany so he can truthfully call himself an Albanian.